Add Years to Your Life & Life to Your Years

Ben Sweetland, Ph.D.
with additional material by
Cathy Stucker
IdeaLady.com

Special Interests Publishing
SUGAR LAND, TEXAS

Contents

A Note From the Publisher

This classic book by Dr. Ben Sweetland has been out of print for many years, and is consequently hard to find. When I heard about it, though, I immediately set about tracking down a copy. I couldn't wait to read it, and the book did not disappoint.

Dr. Sweetland's enthusiasm and positive attitude shine through on every page. The concepts he presents in these pages inspired me to take action to add more life to my years and, I hope, more years to my life.

I knew that I had to bring Dr. Sweetland's words to a new audience of readers. The result is the book you hold in your hands.

Although the ideas in this book do not go out of style, changes in writing styles and society at large made some aspects of the book seem dated. We did not alter Dr. Sweetland's ideas, but we have made some alterations and edits in order to update the book for modern readers.

I have also added some additional material to each section to guide you in implementing Dr. Sweetland's ideas.

Don't just read this book. Use it to make positive change in your life.

Enjoy!

Cathy Stucker
Publisher
Special Interests Publishing

More Youth to Age

Are we developing into a "nation of elders"? It may be so if we realize how many more people are nowadays reaching an advanced age (say over sixty-five) than ever before. This is due to the great advances medicine has made in the last few decades. New problems now exist, unknown or negligible even fifty years ago. How are we to deal with those who are arbitrarily retired from their jobs? Who is to care for those that are no longer able to work and may suffer from infirmities and illnesses? How can the aged themselves cope with their frequent loneliness and with an often hopeless and unhappy frame of mind? It is apparent from these remarks that the problems of old age are threefold. First, sociological; second, medical; and third, psychological.

Dr. Sweetland, in his present volume, deals with the third one only. In his charming, optimistic manner, he gives wise counsel and describes methods of thinking and acting that should prove eminently helpful for a great many people.

Dr. Sweetland's recommendations are based on experience, common sense, and on the power of the mind over the body. Since this power is undeniable and dynamic, the advice contained in the following pages can have, for many of our middle-aged and old, a remarkable and lasting benefit. It employs effectively the principles of psychosomatic medicine.

"Youth" is a state of mind that may exist in an old as well as a young person, just as "being old" may have nothing to do with birthday anniversaries. Yet, our general concept of "youth" and "old age" is well established through customary thinking. Giving more youth to old age is an ever present wish. Every promise toward its fulfillment—even if such is only partial—is eagerly welcomed. Dr. Sweetland shows a way in his new book (a worthy companion to his "I Can") by which much dissatisfaction and much suffering during the later years of life can be made quite unnecessary.

As the title of the present volume, Dr. Sweetland has chosen a phrase which this preface-writer employed over thirty years ago in a medical article entitled "The Control of Old Age" (American Medicine, June, 1927). A prideful gratification may therefore be understandable.

The treatment of the aging process itself is known in medicine as gerontotherapy. It is to be differentiated from geriatrics, which deals with problems of old age in general and in particular with its distinctive and inherent diseases. In other words, gerontotherapy is more concerned with the individual and with adding life to years, while geriatrics primarily treats diseases and organs, adding more years to life. Dr. Sweetland's psychological recommendations fall distinctly into the field of gerontotherapy. It can well supplement other methods employed in this new medical specialty, for instance, glandular treatments, physiotherapy, dietary measures, vitamin medication, etc.

Dr. Sweetland's psychotherapy of aging can show the way for many people to deal successfully with a period of life that is only too often the "winter of discontent" when it could well be the pleasant "autumn of fulfillment."

Psychotherapy, however, is not all that is contained in the following pages. There is also a philosophy. At the turn of the century, a German professor of Philosophy, Hans Vaihinger, originated his

"Philosophy of the As If" ("Die Philosophic des Als Ob"). He advocated a method of thinking that fictionalizes life. He recommended an approach to life's problems "as if" they were different and more acceptable than what cold realism would make them appear. Dr. Sweetland has now independently developed a method of psychological guidance that reminds us of Vaihinger's abstract philosophy but puts it to beneficent and practical use.

It is ardently to be hoped that many people will delve into these pages and draw from them wisdom, satisfaction, and better mental and physical health.

CHAPTER 1

Live As Though Your Life Would Go on Forever

You have a surprise in store for you!

As you saw the title to this book, many questions came to your mind.

Is it another one of those "health faddist's" books which will talk in terms of blackstrap molasses and brewer's yeast, which will attempt to create an impression that long life could be found in a bottle?

Will it prescribe a rigid diet of uninteresting, unpalatable foods, and a warning to detour around anything that might be enjoyable?

Must one adhere to a routine of physical exercises which makes getting up in the morning dreaded instead of anticipated?

No! No! Absolutely No!

This book is built on the theory that...

You would not want to add years to your life if your added years would see you in a state of senility and infirmity.

You must have an incentive to want to add years to your life, and as you pass into the 40's, 50's, 60's and beyond, you will not dread the passing of time, but will welcome each coming hour for the happiness and peace of mind it brings to you.

This book is not written specifically for older people; it is not written for younger people or middle-aged people. It is written for you, no matter who you are or where you are. It is written for those who are young, for those who want to stay young, and for those who would like to turn their calendars back and face a future of promise; a future that shows the same rosy glow as it comes over the horizon that we see in our mind's eye as we look back over our youth—which has faded with the passing of time.

As I start this book, I have reached my 70th birthday; three score years and ten. I should die this coming year, if the 10th verse of the 90th chapter of Psalms applies to me. But, according to my mental alertness, my strength and agility, this earth, and those upon it, will have to put up with my presence for many, many years to come. I doubt if, when at the age of forty, I could have withstood the routine I am now following every day. And, I was considered in good health when I was forty.

Today I have no consciousness of age, nor do I have any fear of the passing of time.

I think I have discovered many secrets of longevity. They are keeping me young, and the scores of men and women who are living according to my way of life are getting the same results.

Before you proceed further, I wish to lay down a few hard and fast rules for you to follow; and for your own sake, follow them.

Do not read this book hastily as you would a novel. Get yourself located where you will not be disturbed and then relax, mentally and physically. Read the book slowly and thoughtfully.

Do not think of the countless thousands of others who might be reading this book. Imagine that it was written for you only, and that every word was intended only for you.

As you read each page, do not merely agree with me that the thoughts are sound; put them to work. Apply them to your own life—now.

Are you in accord with me? All right, let's get started!

Although every suggestion; every instruction; every principle will be of importance, the thought now presented to you will prove to be the keystone of all thoughts to come. Unless you follow this first instruction—right to the letter—you will fail to get the maximum good from this book; and that would not make me a bit happy.

Live as though your life would go on forever!

Sounds simple, doesn't it? In fact, there was a bit of a letdown as you read it. You expected something with far more oomph in it. Right? Well, my dear reader, as this principle is explained, you will appreciate its significance and the dynamic power behind it.

As an illustration: Suppose you are, let us say, in your fifties. A business opportunity comes to you, one which could take several years to develop. With the type of age-consciousness most people have, you would be inclined to look at the proposal with disfavor, feeling you were too old to tackle it. You might even say: "I like the idea, and if it had come to me ten years ago, I would have taken it without hesitation."

Suppose you were living as though your life would go on forever, would you hesitate? Not if you really did like the proposition offered.

How about symptoms of age? Isn't it natural to correlate one's feelings with the calendar? As one grows older he becomes inclined to interpret his pains and aches as indications of old age.

If he is living as though his life would go on forever, and he got a pain or an ache, he would at once realize that in some particular instance he had violated a law of nature and he would search for the cause of the pain or ache and would correct it, thereby restoring that glad-to-be-well feeling.

Later in this book you will learn how our thinking is reflected in our bodies. You will learn why thoughts of aging create physiological changes in the body which actually hasten age. Right now, however, I want to sell you on an idea. I want to offer reason after reason showing you the soundness of my suggestion that you begin living as though your life would go on forever.

Please let me say right here that your life will not go on forever, at least in your present physical body. I believe firmly that, according to God's great plan of life, it was intended that we pass through a cycle of life on this plane, then ascend to whatever is awaiting up in the great beyond. But I do believe, as I will attempt to prove to you in this book, that through our type of thinking and living, we leave this plane of existence far earlier than we should. I also firmly believe that it is not only possible to add many, many years to our lives, but that we can feel vibrantly alive; mentally and physically until we reach the time to make our exit from this glorious earth.

It is now beginning to dawn upon you that it would be wonderful if you could develop a frame of mind whereby you could live as though your life would go on forever. Let us think of some of the advantages of such a mental concept. I'll put down a few which occur to me. You'll think of others, I am sure.

You will not be quick in accepting failure. If you have not yet realized your dreams, you will not give up in despair, feeling it is too late to start over.

You will seek new trails to blaze. Your future will be a continuous exciting adventure, instead of just retirement with nothing to do except to see yourself grow old and senile.

Naturally your health will be good. Instead of worrying about the many ailments one expects with oncoming age; with no age-consciousness you will hold thoughts of effervescing health, and with such thoughts, you just can't help feeling good.

You will not fear the passing of time. Clocks will merely be conveniences enabling you to properly space your activities; not reminders that your life is growing shorter.

Fear of death hastens death. With the thought that your life will go on forever, there will be no tear of death. This, in itself will add years to your life and will also (as given in the expression coined by Dr. Harry Benjamin) add life to your years. You will be happier than you otherwise would. Chapter Eight is devoted to an understanding regarding the fear of death.

To merely suggest that you accept the thought that your life will go on forever would do you little, if any, good. Your present thinking regarding age is the result of thoughts you have accepted over a lifetime. You learn in childhood that people grow old and die. Your thoughts regarding people are always associated with age. You think of them as young, middle-aged and old. And, when you think of them as being old, you associate them with thoughts of senility and death.

So, we have work to do. It will be pleasant work, however, because each step you take toward your objective will bring you added happiness. As you gain the genuine feeling that your life will go on forever, you will sense the impression one gets when he views a gorgeous, varicolored sunrise. It will be like the gods are granting you a new lease on life, and that, no matter what your present chronological age might be, your psychological, or mental age is just beginning.

You will always be surrounded with age-conscious people. You will not be able to prevent yourself from hearing remarks about age, infirmity and death. But, through self-discipline, you can shield yourself from impressions which would otherwise be made on both your conscious and sub-conscious mind.

In former days, radio reception was often marred through interference from all motorized mechanisms, atmospheric conditions, etc. Science developed shields which, when properly installed in your instrument, would bring in the voice or music quite free from static.

You will develop a mental shield which will dissolve all power from everything you see, hear or read regarding old age. If you were told that you could make the greatest dream of your life come true, merely by the expenditure of a bit of pleasant effort, you would not hesitate a moment. The little voice from within would cry out: "Let's go!"

I am about to lay out a routine for you to follow which will enable you to build the new consciousness regarding life, a routine which can easily prove to be the most important step you have ever taken in your life. Every forward move you have ever made was intended to give you happiness or well-being—or both—as an end result. Can you name anything more important than a regime which will add years—many years—to your life; and make all of your remaining years happier?

Before beginning with this routine, I want to extract a promise from you; not a promise to me, but to yourself.

If a loved one should accidentally fall into a lake or stream and would appear to be drowning, you wouldn't stand there and meditate, making such statements to yourself as: "Shall I jump in now, or do it later?" "Maybe I couldn't save him anyway, so I'll do nothing." No! You would, without hesitation, free yourself of much of your clothing and jump in.

Taking an illustration on the positive side: If you should discover a chest of precious gems, you wouldn't hesitate in taking possession of it. You would get it right now.

This is the attitude I want you to have with reference to the routine about to be given to you.

I want you to promise yourself that as you read the various steps, you will take action on them. If you'll do this, dear reader, you will go to bed tonight with a happy heart and the spirit of joy which comes into one's heart after he has been given something of great consequence to him.

Do you promise? All right, here is your vow! Repeat it to yourself slowly and solemnly; just like the happy bride-to-be repeats the marriage vow:

I hereby promise myself that I will erase my old consciousness of age, and will hereafter—without thoughts of age—live as though my life would go on forever.

Repeat it to yourself several times, then begin following the suggestions, right to the letter. Lay out your plan of life for the next twenty years, regardless what your present age may be. If you are twenty—or eighty—plan your life for a period of twenty years, almost as though you knew with certainty your life would go on forever.

Have you had a desire to learn one or more foreign languages? Fine! Decide on the languages you wish to learn and plan on getting started.

Have you always wanted to paint? It so, include it among your objectives. Grandma Moses became famous through her paintings, which were not made until she passed the age of eighty.

Do you envy writers of good books? It you enjoy writing, it is an indication that, with proper training, you can write.

So, if you would like to see the day when your name will appear on the cover of a book, or over a magazine article, know, that with your new attitude toward life, you have plenty of time to become proficient as a writer and plan accordingly.

Would you like to establish a business of your own? It is a great satisfaction to know you are your own boss and that everything you do, you are doing for yourself. If a business of your own is your objective, begin deciding on the type of business you want, then take steps toward making it a reality. (It will help if you will read Chapter Seventeen of my book: I CAN!)

Step Number 1, therefore, is to plan your life several years—twenty at least—in the future. Do so with perfect confidence that your plans will be carried out. Do not, in any way, associate your plans with age. Remember! Your life will go on forever.

Motion creates emotion! Every time you find an age thought coming into consciousness, dispel it with a counter-thought: "My life will go on forever."

In the beginning, when making this affirmation, an under-thought might inform you that it is not true, and of course it isn't in our common sense world, however, some great minds state that there is no such thing as death, we in time disrobe from our present physical bodies and move on to other planes of existence.

I can't overestimate the value of the suggestion being made in this step. When you reach that point where you feel (not wish) that your life will go on and on, things will begin to happen. You will accept new assignments with enthusiasm, instead of feeling: "My time is running out—there is little use to start anything new."

Develop an enthusiasm for life. Learn to love everything about life; human, animal and still life. Keep yourself fascinated over the trees, flowers, streams, sunrises and sunsets. As you see and enjoy the handiworks of nature, be happy that you will be here to admire it—from now on.

Talk to your friends about your new attitude toward life. Lend them your copy of this book; present them with a copy, or urge them to buy a copy for themselves. To get your friends living as you do means they will be with you, instead of trying to dissuade you.

It wouldn't be a bad idea to form a little group among your friends for monthly discussions on the subject of geriatrics. Do not confine your meetings to the contents of this book alone; although it should be the foundation of your work. All material you find on the subject of longer life should be brought before your members for consideration.

Be Happy. It is much easier to think in terms of a long life when you are happy, than when you are otherwise.

When one is "down in the dumps" he doesn't even care if his life will be a long one, in fact, many times he wishes he were dead and away from his earthly troubles. As you become imbued with the thought that "your life will go on forever" reverses will not disturb you, because you are not living with an "it's later than you think" philosophy. You instinctively feel that you have plenty of time to straighten out whatever it might be which is causing you distress. In fact, with the right mental attitude, reverses are blessings in disguise. We grow through our obstacles. To have a set-back, and be able to offset it, is a big satisfaction. We have not only overcome that which had temporarily blocked us, but, through the experience, we have learned how to cope with a similar problem in the future, should another one confront us.

The last step, therefore, in the development of a new conscious-ness regarding our lifespan can be summed up in two words: Be Happy!

A great philosopher once said that not more than one person out of four is capable of grasping a new idea. This I do not accept, literal-ly. I do believe that not more than one person out of four attempts to grasp a new idea. One listening to, or reading of, a new idea, will do so with passive interest. He might admit that the idea seems to have merit, but there he stops. He does nothing about it.

The one intent on self-improvement will, after learning of an idea of merit, first ask himself: "How does this apply to me?" If he finds the idea does fit in with his life as he wishes to make it, he will begin at once to take steps to make use of the idea.

It is my sincere hope that the readers of this book come from the 25% of people, those last referred to. Since writing the book I CAN, I have received thousands of letters from those who claim their lives have been transformed by following the suggestions contained in the book. I want to receive the same kind of a reward from this book. It will make me most happy to hear from you, telling me that by apply-ing the principles as given, you are outwitting Father Time, and are getting more out of life than you ever thought possible.

How Are Your Finances?

Insecurity, perhaps, is one of the most common reasons for fear of old age. If one's future does not appear secure, he is most likely to dread the coming of old age, due to the mental pictures of the dire things which can happen to him; particularly the thought of becom-ing dependent upon others.

Fearing the arrival of old age will hasten the effects which age can bring. None of us can stop the movement of time. We can hide the calendars and stop the clocks—but —Time Marches On! We can, however, postpone the "ravages" of old age by developing the correct attitude toward ourselves in relation to time.

Should you, by chance, be one of the many affected by a feeling of insecurity, know that, by adopting the regime outlined in this book, you will be preparing yourself, mentally and physically, to cope with any situation which might arise.

According to insurance statistics, the average person will climb— financially—until he reaches the age of fifty. He then levels off for a while and after that descends quite rapidly. In other words, it he has not attained his security by the time he is fifty, there is little chance left for him to do so.

If I may use myself as an example, since I reached the fifties, I not only went broke but found myself many thousands of dollars in debt. This was at a time when, according to the tables of averages, I should be through; I should go down for the count, so to speak. It was at the time when I began to seriously think about age. I admit I was panicky for a time. It would have been next to impossible to get a job which would enable me to get out of the woods and provide for a future. In the first place, good jobs for one in the fifties were not available.

"Live as though your life would go on forever," was the thought which came to me. "Why not?"

I had been a student of mind since my early twenties. I knew much about the mind and how it operates. I understood how negative thinking would cause negative reactions, and I also understood how positive thinking would bring about positive reactions.

The advantages of "living as though life went on forever" were obvious. It would at once take away fear of the future, because with such a philosophy, there would be all the future one would want for great accomplishment.

What happened to me was little short of being miraculous. Instead of feeling "it is later than you think" I began to believe I had all the time there was. Without an awareness of pressure, I calmly analyzed my situation, worked out a plan, and it was but a short time before I was making great strides. I not only liquidated my indebtedness in short order, but built a business which gives me a genuine sense of security regarding the future.

What I accomplished actually added spice to my life. It gave me a sense of achievement—which made me grow mentally and spiritually. It gave me a new respect for myself, and built within me a courage which makes me unafraid of any future situation which could or might arise.

A skeptical person is usually considered to be a negative person. This is not always true. I feel that skepticism, if backed by investigation, is constructive.

You were promised that, by following the teachings in this book, you would live a longer, healthier and happier life. Such a promise could easily arouse the skepticism of any thinking person. A long, healthy, happy life is so cherished by all, it would seem doubtful that the mere reading of a book would make this condition a reality. Of course, it is doubtful that the mere reading of the book would bring such a Utopian condition about. As I have implied so far in this book, in order to add zestful years to your life, you must work at it. The words you read provide you with the blueprint from which you work. And, here, permit me to soften the impression you might get from the word "work."

The word "work" as intended means the application of the rules and suggestions as given.

Summary

The gist of this entire chapter can be summed up in the statement given so frequently: Live As Though Your Life Would Go on Forever!

Make the commitment that you will start living as though your life would go on forever:

I hereby promise myself that I will erase my old consciousness of age, and will hereafter—without thoughts of age—live as though my life would go on forever.

Plan the next 20 years of your life. What will you do differently, now that you are living as though your life would go on forever? Will you change careers, start a business, write a book, build your dream house?

As a constructive suggestion, before starting Chapter Two, reread this one. This time read a page or two at a time—then pause. Think over what you have read to make certain you are retaining it, then proceed.

I can't overestimate the importance of what has so far been given to you. And, what you get out of the entire book depends largely on what you get out of the first chapter.

Now then, make of this book the vanguard of a new life; new aspirations; new happiness.

CHAPTER 2

Developing the Urge to Want to Live Longer

"I do not want to add years to my life!" declared a woman who had been discussing longevity with me.

She was in her sixties; was not in too good health, and had just buried a father of 85 who had spent his last years in suffering and senility.

"Would you like to add years to your life," I asked, "if you could feel good physically; regain the spark of youth, and face your lengthened future with an alert mind and active body?"

"Naturally I would," she smiled. "Who wouldn't?"

This conversation, and many others like it, revealed an interesting truth.

When people claim they would not like to prolong their lives, they do not mean that at all. They are afraid of old age. The very words "old age" connotes to them mental pictures of canes, crutches, wheelchairs, confinement in bed, etc. They think of tottering, feeble men and women who are not living, but merely existing. Hanging on, waiting for Father Time to catch up with them.

If I could foresee such a future for myself, I would not want to live to a "ripe old age." I definitely believe that the best in this life does not slightly compare with what awaits us as we travel to higher planes. Why should I, then, want to postpone my advancement, if doing so would mean boredom and suffering?

This book is intended to show the way to live a brilliant life; mentally alert and physically strong and well.

So, the theme of this chapter will be: Developing the Urge to Want to Live Longer.

When I say: Developing the Urge to Want to Live Longer, I do not in any way mean wishing to live longer.

"I already have the urge," you might say, "especially if my longer life would see me well and happy."

This is not enough. One can readily say he has the urge without fully comprehending the significance of the statement he is making. Study the meaning of the word "urge" and you'll understand what I mean. Webster defines the word by saying: "To force onward; prosecute energetically. To force or impel in an indicated direction, especially onward; to drive."

When you have the urge to do anything, you permit nothing to stand in your way; to stand between you and the attainment of whatever it was that gave you the urge.

If you are still reading this book, it is an evidence of interest. You would like to grow younger and add years to your life. At least you are curious to find out if you can grow younger, and if it would be worth your while to try.

If this is the case, you are not yet on the right track. We never try to do the things we know we can do. To say you will try to do anything is an evidence of your doubt that you can do it, otherwise you would not have to try.

What, then, is the best way to develop an urge to want to live longer? Wouldn't it be to find an incentive; a valid reason as to why you should live longer in order to properly enjoy your incentive?

Let's do a little supposing. Imagine yourself living in an ordinary city apartment. You learn that some of your friends have become imbued with the do-it-yourself spirit—even to the extent of building their own homes.

You do not get very excited over the thought of a do-it-yourself home, thinking that it would plainly show that it was constructed by unskilled hands.

You are invited to visit one of these homes, and to your utter surprise the home is most attractive; extremely livable, and, above all, reflects the personality of the couple who built it.

You are seized with a desire to do the same thing yourself. You would thoroughly enjoy acquiring a lot, a set of do-it-yourself plans; and, after adding some of your own ideas to the plans, proceeding to build your home. Your desire is not so much due to large possible savings, but for the thrill which comes when you can listen to your friends rave about the home you built.

There are barriers, however, standing between you and the attainment of this objective. You have no money with which you could buy the plot of ground, nor the building materials to construct the house.

But, and here is where the potency of the principles contained in this book is concerned. Suppose you knew you could regain a youthful spirit and that you did not have to dread the coming of birthdays, would you hesitate taking the necessary steps to convert this desire into a reality? No! You would select the plot of ground you desire; perhaps that one on the hilltop you have always admired, but never thought it could be yours. Since the passing of time does not matter, you save until you get the down payment. Through your resourcefulness, you find ways and means of earning extra money to hasten the day when the plot will be yours. While doing this, you spend your spare time in studying plans, and, perhaps, add your own ideas here and there.

You see? Doesn't such an incentive tie right in with the principles being given in this book? Should this be your incentive, you would happily visualize yourself building such a home. You would gain in physical strength, because you would know that with such a project you simply must be in the pink of condition—and you would not be able to see yourself in any other way.

But, building a home is not the only incentive. No siree! There are many of them. They extend to the limit of your imagination.

How about travel? Have you envied those who have travelled around the world, visiting many of the most interesting countries? You might have felt that this is one pleasure you have missed and that you are "too far along in years" to consider such a move. But, ah-ah, all such thinking predates the time of the discovery of the proved principles you are now learning. So, make travel an incentive.

It might take a year or two before you can get your affairs in shape and, perhaps, the necessary money in your pockets, to enable you to take a month or two for such a project. So what? Time means nothing in your life. Your new philosophy of life is taking years off your looks and is adding them to your life.

Between now and the time you start your trip, you can have lots of fun reading travel folders. Get a good travel agent to lay out your trip for you and supply you with literature regarding the many countries you will visit. It doesn't matter if it will be a few months or over a year before your departure. Every idle moment will be joyously spent in preparation for the coming trip. If you have an encyclopedia, you may wish to read about the various continents you will visit. You will learn about the people, their customs, and their languages. You will read about the weather in each place at the time of your visit so that you can be provided with proper wearing apparel.

Would you like to learn one or more languages? You have the time, so, if you have the inclination, what are you waiting for?

"Oh, how I wish I could paint," sighed a woman as she eyed many of the fine canvasses in an art gallery. "Why don't you?" I asked.

"I? Why I'm too old to take up anything like that. Next month I will be 48," she admitted remorsefully.

To anyone with the right attitude toward age, 48 is the prime of life.

A close friend of mine had never had a brush in his hand until after he had past the age of 50. He took up painting as a hobby, and before he reached 60, had had several of his paintings on exhibition.

Can you become excited over the prospect of becoming a good landscape or portrait painter? Forget your chronological age and make a start. Use painting as an incentive.

One of the most common regrets of those who have passed the so-called middle-age is that they did not go into a business for themselves. They see others who have built up successful businesses and who can take plenty of time off to enjoy their yachts and country clubs.

In my own case, I established a business after I had passed the age of 60. I can't tell you the thrill I am getting as I watch it grow. Although looking after my business, and writing and lecturing, I have very little time for leisure, I am enjoying life to its utmost. Clocks and calendars mean nothing to me—except as a manner of apportioning my time.

In San Francisco lives a little lady who has just entered the 80's. She recently started a business of manufacturing and marketing a beauty aid.

When asked if she is not a bit too far along in life to tackle such a responsibility, she indignantly replies: "Too old your foot! I'm getting the kick of my life out of what I am doing. It keeps me young."

If you aspire to head a business of your own, notwithstanding the number of years you have been on this plane of existence, decide you will become your own boss.

Start making your plans and get yourself so excited over the prospects of a business you will declare that you must live a long and healthful life so that you can succeed in putting it over.

A Plan of Life

Have you begun to realize that you are not merely reading a book? No! You are laying out a plan of life. You are accepting a new philosophy by which you will live. Your attitude toward age—as it applies to you—is changing completely.

For a moment I would like to address a few remarks to those who have accepted the thought that they are old. What I say will be of interest to those of all ages, however. If you are in the 20's or 30's, fine. You will learn something which you can pass on to that grandfather who has begun to think of himself as an old man.

Throughout this fine land of ours are many clubs and organizations intended to be of help to the seniors, as they often refer to men and women past 60.

The intentions are good, but stay away from them. There is nothing which will give you a consciousness of age more than a club which was formed to be of help to those well along in years.

Such clubs are thought of as "Old People's Clubs." The organizers had very good intentions, but the feeling is: "These poor souls haven't many more years to live and we ought to do all we can to make their last years happy." Heck! Would you like to be a part of such a movement? If your answer is "yes" you had better stop reading this book right now, because it will do you but little good.

You're not going to join any "Old Folks Gang!" because you are not old, no matter what your birth certificate might say. You are young in spirit and will soon be noticing a return of youth to your physical being.

I have visited many groups made up of "oldsters." All who attend, do so as sort of watchers for old Father Time who are trying to keep a stiff upper lip until he arrives.

Please do not feel I am cruel in the attitude I am taking regarding movements which have started with the finest of intentions. I am appraising them from a psychological standpoint. They do render a service in the way of giving those who have looked at themselves as being elderly, something to do to pass away time. But they do not send a man or woman home with the feeling: "I am growing younger." Do they? You answer that question.

I want you to become so occupied—mentally, particularly—that instead of looking for means of whiling away time, you will do everything within your power to conserve time.

Age Is Largely Psychosomatic!

Since such authorities as the late Dr. John A. Schindler tell us that 70% of all ailments are psychosomatic, we can safely assume that the condition we refer to as old age is also, to a large extent, psychosomatic.

The time will come when an age of 125 years will no longer be an exception, but the rule.

After one passes 50, he begins to feel he is getting on the "old" side—and lives accordingly. He interprets all of his aches and pains in terms of age.

When young, an ache or pain would indicate that he had violated a law of nature and he would do something to correct the condition. In later life, nothing is done because he considers such maladies belong to one of his years.

I am repeating these thoughts at this time, because I want to impress upon you the importance of developing the right impression regarding age. The success you will have with this book will depend largely on how thoroughly you accept the suggestions given in these first two chapters.

Are you excited? Are you now visualizing a future of happy accomplishment, and with a body vibrantly alive? That is the mental pattern I want you to have. And, if you haven't that feeling, it is because you have not focused your thoughts on that which you have been reading. If, by chance this does apply to you, please stop at the end of this chapter and reread the first two chapters. And read them slowly and thoughtfully.

If you are excited, then you may proceed with Chapter Three which will raise your interest to still higher levels.

Summary

This chapter is intended to give you the urge to want to live longer.

If you have taken everything seriously, and applied the suggestions to yourself, instead of feeling they are thoughts broadcast to the multitudes, you not only want to live longer, but are determined to do so.

Start associating with like-minded people, and avoid negative ideas about aging.

Give yourself an incentive to live a long life by imagining doing the things in your 20-year plan.

Do not dwell on the end—enjoy the journey.

CHAPTER 3

Gaining Awareness That Through Proper Living and Correct Thinking One CAN Add Years to His Life!

What have we learned so far? In the first chapter we learned that one should live as though his life would go on forever. We next learned that a person, in order to add years to his life, must first desire to do so, so you were urged to find an incentive to want to live longer.

Assuming you have accepted the thoughts so far given, you want to be convinced that, through proper living and correct thinking, you can add years to your life. Therefore, this chapter will not only tell you that you can add years to your life, but will tell you why you should.

In my younger days I operated an advertising agency. Whenever I was approached to create an advertising campaign, I began by making a study of the product to determine whether or not it had marketable possibilities. In making my study I would first tear it down, negatively, considering every bad point I could think of. If the proposition still stood up after such antithetical scrutiny, it was proper to conclude it had much merit, and I then would assume the responsibility of developing a campaign.

Let us, for a moment, view the statements I have been making from a negative standpoint to see if they still stand up.

Suppose I am "all wet" in my theories regarding the regaining of youth, and the prolongation of life. If you can keep your mind free from thoughts of death and fear of old age, won't your remaining years be happier? Of course they will. And, since it is an established fact that worry and fear make one grow old faster, we must conclude that, by eliminating all thoughts in connection with the passing of time, we will live longer and, most certainly regain much of our lost youth.

I was giving a broadcast over a New York radio station. My subject was: Youth and How to Retain It. I asked my listeners to join with me in an experiment. I suggested that each listener over forty should deduct ten years from his age. If one was 52, for example, he should see himself as 42. I urged my radio friends to live as though they were 10 years younger, and imagine that to be their true ages. They should dress as the younger person; they should do the things which a person ten years younger would normally do.

After a month letters began coming in from those who were experimenting with me.

"My friends are asking me what I did to make myself look younger," one listener wrote. "I feel younger, and have more energy than I did before trying your experiment," wrote another.

"Since 'becoming younger,'" declared an experimenter, "I am increasing the number of sales I am making. I seem to have taken on a new lease on life."

And so went the letters. Amazing results from such a simple experiment.

This brought back to memory a psychological experiment tried with an illiterate man who had passed the age of 70. Getting him all confused regarding dates, he was made to believe he was 10 years

younger than he actually was. Immediately he began looking younger. He was more physically active than he had been for many years.
In short, he began looking the part of a man 10 years his junior.

Later the deceived man discovered the hoax, and it was only days
before he looked, acted and thought like he did before the deception.

Thoughts Make Us Old; They Can Make Us Young

Very few people fully realize the force of thought. It works in
both directions. The one with a negative mind (and studies show
that nine out of ten people lean toward the negative side) is constantly creating negative conditions in the body through negative
thoughts. Thoughts of aging are among the most destructive types
of thinking.

Permit me to tell you a few stories to illustrate my point. A Cali-
fornia resident, in her 80's desired to take a trip to New York to visit
a married son. She thought her time was running out and she felt
she should take the trip while she was alive to do so. A son, also a
resident of the Pacific Coast volunteered to take her east. This little
mother's health had not been too good because her attention had
been focused on age, rather than health. She was constantly told:
"Don't do this or that on account of your age"; "Don't eat this or
don't eat that, they are not good for you"; etc., etc. The son, who was
a positive thinker, secured a drawing room on the train, and as it
steamed out of Oakland, heading east, he told his mother: "On this
trip, mother, you are not to think of a thing except happy things.
Not a word will be discussed about health—except good health."

During the trip, no comments were made regarding ailments of
any kind, but the son frequently did tell his mother how much better
and brighter she looked. Hour by hour, day by day, this little mother
grew better and better. She ate whatever appealed to her; she slept
soundly at night (although before starting, she was sure she could

not sleep on a train). When she stepped off the train at Grand Central Station in New York, she was twenty years younger in attitude, looks and actions than before starting her journey.

The married son she intended visiting, lived quite a distance from New York City, so the mother decided to see the "big town" for a few days, staying with another relative who lived in Manhattan.

During those days in New York, this octogenarian was on the go every minute; sight-seeing trips, dinners, shows, etc. And she felt fine.

But, and here comes the unhappy part of this story.

The wife of the son she visited was a trained nurse before her marriage. Her background had been treating the sick. So, mother was put on a routine. "Don't eat this!" "Don't do that," etc. Within a week, this precious soul was confined to her bed. When her thoughts were focused on health and well-being, her health and spirits were improved, immeasurably. As soon as her thoughts were directed toward age—and the illnesses one is expected to have at such later time in life, her body began reflecting the negative condition.

A woman in the 40's had been gaining quite an age complex. She had lost her secretarial position, and every time she would apply for a job was told she was too old. Each time she would peer at her reflection in the mirror she'd look for signs of age and find them, because she had been putting them there.

I tried an experiment with her, using hypnosis as a means of influencing her thinking regarding age.

The trend of our thinking is based upon the pattern established in the subconscious mind. If that is negative, it is difficult for the conscious mind to do anything except hold thoughts leaning toward the negative, or destructive side. In the case of the lady in question, she had so often been told she was too old, she had subconsciously accepted the thought she was old. She became old in thought, actions and looks.

In hypnosis, the hypnotist brings on a condition of induced sleep, then he talks to the subconscious mind— which never sleeps.

Putting this young woman into a hypnotic sleep, I talked to her subconscious mind in terms of youth. I told her that she was young and that she couldn't see herself as anything but young. "When you go to the mirror," I told her, "you will look for signs of youth." I implanted thoughts regarding relaxation to relieve the tension she had been expressing and left thoughts of restful sleep.

All right, what happened? Her new mental attitude began to reflect itself in her looks and in her physical being. She later applied for a position with a firm that chose to hire vibrant young employees. This woman looked so much younger than her real age, the firm gave her a good position.

Thoughtless remarks about "getting old" do much damage to one's physical being, and—they are altogether too often responsible for an age-complex.

"Be your age"; "You're too old for this or that"; "Take care of yourself, you know you are not as young as you used to be" are a few of the thoughtless remarks made to those who might be a bit along in years. They do tremendous damage. As you will learn in later chapters, when we accept such thoughts we begin aging quite rapidly, and often prematurely.

I do hope that the readers of this book will refrain from making such remarks, and will do all they can to prevent others from speaking thoughtlessly.

A widowed mother came to me for a helpful thought. She was not particular about getting married again, but she was lonely. She had two daughters in their late teens, but they never took their mother with them. When the mother hinted that she would enjoy going places with the girls, she was always put in her place with a remark such as: "Aw gee, ma, it's no fun going out with an old lady, why don't you read, or knit, or something?"

This woman, although not more than 45 years of age did look old. She had so thoroughly accepted the thought that she was old, she did nothing to make herself look otherwise. Her hair was smoothed back, she used no make-up and wore dresses which were colorless and which definitely accentuated her age.

The age of 45 is not old. As a matter of fact, a woman of 45, if she knows how to keep her spark of youth, is more interesting than most of the younger women. She not only has the mind and body of youth but, in addition, has had sufficient years to gain the experiences which enable her to be far more entertaining than one of fewer years.

My wife, an actress of note, knows much about dress and make-up. I asked her to counsel with my visitor, showing her how to make herself look more attractive. I had already given her a good lecture regarding her mind and the important part it plays in making her old, or keeping her young.

Between the two of us, my wife and I, we transformed the woman from a drab old widow to an active scintillating and really young person.

What effect did this have on the two daughters? You can easily guess. Now they are proud of their mother. They are always including her in their parties, and enjoy introducing her to their friends. And this is not all. I am certain you'll make another correct guess. Yes, this fine woman not only became popular with her two girls, but is now happily wearing a gorgeous engagement ring.

This forty-five year old woman, when first coming to me, looked and acted well over her age. Now she looks and acts and feels many years younger than her actual age.

A man of fifty-four found himself without a position because the firm for which he worked went out of business. All doors to employment were closed to him on account of his age. What an age-complex he developed. He felt that life had ended so far as he was concerned and, as he confessed to me later, he had been planning on ending his own life.

"Since you can't get a job, why don't you go into business for yourself?" I inquired.

"A business of my own—and without money?" he chided.

"If you have the I CAN spirit," I retorted good humoredly, "You can establish a business of your own—and without initial capital."

I explained that there were many magazines for salesmen, brimming with opportunities of securing franchises for the sale of various commodities, many of which may be secured without an investment.

A middle-aged man, without money, obtained a territory for the sale of a specialty. He started out doing all the selling himself. After he got a bit of income flowing in, he employed a few salesmen to sell under him. He now has a staff of at least 10 men; has an office, and, I dare say is making an excellent salary.

This fifty-four year old man who had been licked through circumstances stared out of the window in deep thought.

"I think you have something there," he, at last drawled, and calmly so.

I picked up a copy of a salesman's magazine which had been lying on my desk. Together we thumbed through the pages, turning down the comers of those pages which seemed to hold something of interest.

"Write to a few of these concerns," I suggested, and select the one which comes nearest to arousing your genuine enthusiasm.

"While waiting for the material to arrive," I urged, "get yourself in the right frame of mind regarding your age." And, repeating the thought, outlined in Chapter 1, I extracted a promise that "he would live as though his life would go on forever."

Without dragging this story too far, permit me to tell you that this man is now making more money than he had ever made in his life.

"Losing my job was a blessing in disguise," he confided as we sat down to lunch in a fine downtown hotel. Incidentally, he insisted on paying for the lunch—an expensive one—whereas when I first met him it would have strained his resources to take me to a hot-dog stand.

Coming back to you, my good reader, are you beginning to gain the feeling that one can grow younger—and live longer? I sense that you are. When talking on this subject to audiences, I am inspired as I watch the changes coming over the faces as members of the audience realize that age is largely a matter of consciousness, and, that one is not truly old—until he accepts the thought of old age.

Are We Resorting to Self-Deception?

Many illustrations have been given—showing how one will actually grow young through a change of mental attitude. Does this mean that age is just a phantom, and, that all one must do is to shake himself out of the delusion and he will rebound to a youthful state? Not at all.

The subconscious mind is in direct charge of all operations going on within the body; the breathing, beating of the heart, circulation of the blood, etc.

Every moment of every day tissue is wearing out and being replaced by new tissue. All of this great work comes under the direction of the subconscious mind. There is intelligence in every bodily cell, and this intelligence is part of—and directly associated with—the subconscious mind.

People who have developed an age-consciousness, hold mental pictures of themselves—growing old. They see their bodies taking on the indications of aging; lowered vitality, a general slowing down of all bodily activity. Such conscious mental pictures are accepted as patterns by the subconscious mind which reproduces in the body the conditions pictured in the conscious mind. When we begin holding pictures of youth, vitality, robust health, we are changing the pattern, with the result that we soon begin reflecting the new state of youth we pictured.

To give you an idea of the potency of mental pictures, permit me to relate the story of an experience I once had. My day in the office was very busy, so busy in fact, I entirely forgot to go out for lunch. About 4 o'clock in the afternoon, it occurred to me that I had not eaten. Up to that minute I was not a bit hungry, but as soon as I realized I had not had my lunch, I became ravenously hungry and could hardly wait until I could get to the coffee shop.

I will tell you about an idiosyncrasy of mine. Ever since childhood I have had an antipathy toward cheese of any kind; so strong, that anything even bearing the name of cheese became repugnant to me.

One afternoon I was invited to a home and, during my visit, tea and biscuits were served. The biscuits were delicious; so much so that I ate several of them. The hostess told me it pleased her to have me so enjoy her biscuits, then she proceeded to tell of the new recipe she had used. Cottage cheese was one of the principle ingredients. It may cause you to smile when I say I actually became ill knowing that I had eaten some cheese. Had I not been made aware of the presence of cheese, I probably would have carried away a memory of having enjoyed some extra fine biscuits.

Later in this book you will read much about fatigue, and how most fatigue is psychosomatic—mental. Getting tired because we expect to get tired is another bit of evidence as to the potency of thought and its effects on our bodies. More of mental pictures in Chapter Six.

Summary

This chapter was intended to sell you one idea, that through proper living and correct thinking, one can grow younger and add years to his life.

Think of yourself as 10 years younger than your calendar age. If you are really bold, subtract 20 years! Think, dress and act as if you are younger than your age.

Reject the negative stereotypes of aging. Age does not have to lead to infirmity.

If you are not convinced this is true, before proceeding to the next chapter reread this one, s-l-o-w-l-y and thoughtfully. And then prepare for an enjoyable session with the next one.

CHAPTER 4

Guilt, and Its
Effect on Age

To ask one if he has a guilty conscience is flirting with trouble. He is apt to demand that you either apologize or explain what you mean. Yet, from a psychological standpoint, most everyone has a feeling of guilt due to some kind of an act committed during his lifetime. He might not even remember the act which caused the feeling of guilt, yet he continues paying the price for the indiscretion, and it is usually a very high price.

What has this to do with age? Plenty! A guilt complex causes one to feel—subconsciously—he is not entitled to the good things of life. He may not reason why, but when considering any future experience which could bring great happiness there is an inward feeling that he is not entitled to it, and instead of looking forward to the event, is most likely to feel sorry for himself because it will not be his.

I believe that most failure complexes stem from a guilty conscience. Without being aware why, one with a strong feeling of guilt will accept the fact that "it is just my luck to be a failure."

I believe that most people who are plagued with aches and pains suffer from a feeling of guilt. They just feel Nature did not intend they should enjoy good health.

I believe that most people who show age early in life do so because of that inner feeling of guilt which tells them they are not entitled to retain the blessings of youth.

What Are the Causes of Guilt?

Are feelings of guilt due to big crimes? Murder, stealing, cheating? No, not necessarily at all. Most frequently, a feeling of guilt arises from the most trivial and unimportant acts.

As much as I dislike pointing an accusing finger at the parents, they are responsible for most feelings of guilt their children carry through life.

"You'll never amount to anything," parents will often tell the child who has in some way misbehaved. If this thought is accepted by the subconscious mind, as it often is, the child will reach adulthood with an inner feeling that he is not supposed to be good, and therefore will never have the admiration and respect of those with whom he comes in contact.

A young man in the middle twenties was deeply in love with a girl, but hesitated proposing to her because he considered himself unclean and not worthy of her love. Upon asking him a long series of questions, it was learned that when he was a boy his mother drilled into his young mind that masturbation was one of the worst sins one could commit. This boy—as do many boys—would masturbate. Based upon the preachments of his mother, he'd reached adulthood with very little respect for himself. He considered himself too unclean to have any intimate contact with a wholesome woman.

A woman of my acquaintance had such a guilt complex she dreaded looking at her reflection in the mirror.

"I hate myself," she told me when first coming for counsel. It took quite a bit of reasoning on my part to get her to tell her story; to tell me the things which would enable me to get to the root of her difficulty.

This woman was the daughter of a Puritanical New England mother. According to the mother, any girl who would put liquor to her lips was a bit lower than the low.

The girl grew up and married a man whose custom it was to have a cocktail every evening before dinner. He persuaded his wife to join him, and it wasn't long until she had the habit of imbibing each evening, along with her husband. But, her conscience bothered her. She took the drinks to satisfy her husband, but she couldn't help remembering what her mother had said so often.

When assured that what she had been doing was no different than what countless thousands of respectable women did every day of the week, she finally lost her feeling of guilt and began enjoying life.

The feeling of insecurity that so many people have is usually a hangover from childhood days.

"You take care of those trousers, the Lord only knows when you'll get another pair," is a statement often made to children at play. They are reminded that daddy is not rich; that money does not grow on trees. If a crust of bread is left on the plate, the child is reminded of the thousands of starving people who would love to have that crust, and also that the day might arrive when the child, himself, will wish he had that very same crust of bread. With such early impressions, it is no wonder children grow into adulthood, always with the feeling that poverty lurks around the corner.

One with a guilt complex will instinctively feel that he is not entitled to anything that might be joy to him. This applies particularly to physical well-being. One subconsciously feels that to be jubilant and mentally alert is taking advantage of a condition to which he is not entitled.

You will now understand why I am devoting a chapter to the elimination of any possible guilt complex.

The Power of Forgiveness

Every thinking person will agree that one should be forgiving. If we have wronged someone, we should be big enough to ask forgiveness. If someone has wronged us, we should be big enough to forgive.

There is one person, however, we never think of, when it comes to forgiving; and that person is one's self. Does it seem strange to suggest that you forgive yourself? That body of yours is just as much a part of humanity as the body of anyone else. And, if it is proper to forgive another, why isn't it just as proper to forgive yourself?

There is not a man or woman in the world who has not made mistakes in his or her life. If you will be big enough profit by your mistakes, they can prove to be blessings instead of a hindrance.

I have made lots of mistakes in my life, some of which cause me to blush as I think of them. But instead of permitting them to hold me back through a feeling of guilt, I through my lectures, books and radio talks, have helped thousands of other people to avoid making the same mistakes I made. This being true, doesn't it prove that my mistakes have been a blessing? In fact, in a small way, this world is a better place in which to live, due to my mistakes.

You can profit by your mistakes. Taking the right attitude toward them, you will grow. You will know how to avoid the same kind of mistakes in the future, and of course, you can, as I did, help others to avoid repeating their mistakes.

Before you retire tonight, give serious thought to what you have been reading. See the wisdom of self-forgiveness and act upon it. Go to sleep with a mind of joy and peace. Sense your new happiness since you have cleansed your heart and mind of every semblance of hatred or ill-will you have held against yourself. You will be surprised how much better you will feel tomorrow. No matter how the skies look; whether they be bright or cloudy, there will be a ray of sunshine and happiness in your heart.

As you think about growing young and adding years to your life, there will be no doubt in your mind. You'll rejoice because you know you are growing younger and that you WILL add years to your life.

A young lady came to me for counsel. She had aspired to be a great singer. She had an exceptionally good voice. Her teacher held out great promise for her, yet she never seemed to get anywhere. When giving an audition which could lead her into fame, she would freeze up and could not do herself justice at all.

In talking with her, I found that she was harboring a fully developed guilt complex.

"I'm just bad," she moaned as I was trying to pin her down to specific statements regarding her ill-will toward herself.

She had made mistakes. She admitted a few occasions when she had had intimacies with college students, particularly after having too much to drink. She had frequently lied to her parents as to where she had spent her time when away from home.

She saw no merit at all in my theory regarding forgiving herself. I assured her that to forgive herself, so that she could, with a clear conscience, repeat the sins, would do her no good at all. But, if she could forgive herself because she wanted to live a better and more wholesome life, then by all means do so.

She finally saw the wisdom of my suggestion and agreed to abide by it.

After she had regained her self-respect and created a feeling of self-appreciation, things began to happen.

Facing the future with confidence, instead of remorse, she gave auditions which revealed her true talent. She was given a contract and is now making a very good income as a professional singer.

Subconsciously, this young lady felt she was not entitled to success. Whenever she would try to make good, something within would block her from doing her best. Freed from her sense of guilt, through self-forgiveness, she was able to project her newly found self-appreciation into her singing.

I am sure that many indications of age which reflect in one's face were put there because of feelings of guilt. As one envies younger people and wishes he could be actively young, the little voice from within explains that he is not entitled to be young and carefree.

A man told me what happened to him after he had forgiven himself. He could never get himself in the frame of mind where he would like to indulge in any of the sports enjoyed by other men. He always had some excuse as to why he could not go fishing, or hunting, or golfing; in fact partake in any kind of sport or game. His excuses at the time would seem plausible, but later he would always find that he could have partaken of the pastime, had he wanted to do so.

When I explained the theory of self-forgiveness, his mind raced back to his childhood days, and he recalled the number of times his mother forbade him from going swimming, fishing, hunting, etc., telling him that boys who did such things seldom amounted to much, for having wasted their time. He had, however, stolen opportunities to engage in such sports. In adulthood he was hampered by a feeling of guilt until it was impressed upon him that recreation is just as important as work, and that if one drives himself to work continuously, without time for rest and relaxation, he could easily reach a point where his work would suffer.

This man is now frequently seen on the golf course and he takes time out now and then for a fishing and hunting trip. He enjoys good health, is openly happy, and is making greater progress in his work than he did before.

Sometimes a feeling of guilt will strike one in his physical being. Psychosomatic ailments, as you know, emanate from the mind. Doesn't it, then, seem reasonable to assume that many times aches and pains are subconsciously produced because we do not feel entitled to that glad-to-be-alive feeling?

A man of my acquaintance suffered greatly from pains in his back. He would tire quickly, and at the end of the day was so exhausted he could not enjoy any pleasurable pastime. A search into his childhood revealed the reason for his complex.

Both the mother and father of this man died while he was about 15. They had suffered for several years; but the boy, being on the lazy side, did nothing to help them; even in their poor physical condition. After it was too late, this lad realized how much of their suffering could have been avoided had he helped them. Subconsciously he felt he should suffer in payment for neglecting his parents.

When it was pointed out to this man that it was certain the parents were holding nothing against him, and that if it were possible for them to send a message to him from the other side, it would be asking him to be happy and well. It was also explained that the parents, themselves, were responsible for his laziness due to the manner in which he was reared.

"I know what I'll do," declared this fellow, with a new note of enthusiasm in his voice. "I'll work harder than I ever have worked in an attempt to make a name for myself, all in respect to the memory of my parents."

It was almost a "miraculous healing." Within 24 hours our friend suffered no more pains, and, he found to his pleasant surprise, he had great endurance. He would end each day without fatigue.

Raymond Jones was a failure throughout his life. He was brilliant, industrious, and possessed a most magnetic personality. On the surface it seemed he had all it takes to make an outstanding success. Like the mouse in the bathtub which would climb a few inches, then slip back; Raymond's life was a series of ups and downs. He would make a bit of progress, but before reaching a point of security, would slide back.

Probably this man felt: "It's just my luck to have these things happen," but it wasn't a matter of bad luck at all. It all resulted from a guilt complex.

When a young man, Jones was always running in debt and would always find a way to get out of paying his debts.

In adult life he was subconsciously affected by the manner in which he had treated his creditors. Since he had cheated so many people when he was young, there was an inner feeling to the effect he was not entitled to success.

We are constantly faced with problems, no matter what our objective might be. With this man, whenever a problem would confront him, instead of using his resourcefulness in solving it, would stop in his tracks, feeling, "What's the use? I can't put it over."

Not all of these illustrations pertained to longer life and good health. They were given to show that a feeling of guilt will hold one back from attaining a desired objective.

Summary

True guilt serves a purpose. It alerts us that we have done something wrong, something we should not do again. However, many people carry guilt with them over trivial mistakes or things that were not their fault.

When you have legitimate guilt, learn the lesson it offers, then move on. One way to let go of guilt is to make amends. Pay back the money you took. Apologize to someone you have wronged.

Do not try to relieve your pain by transferring it to someone else. Confessing an affair to your spouse may make you feel better, but your spouse will not feel better having that information.

Forgive yourself. Use the memory of the guilt to avoid actions that hurt others, but stop beating yourself up.

Since it has been established that a feeling of guilt can retard—or even block—the attainment of an objective; and, since most everyone has at least a twinge of a guilt feeling, proceed as though you were certain of possessing one.

Until all feeling of guilt has been eradicated, upon retiring each evening give thanks that you have cleansed your heart and mind of all semblances of hatred or ill-will you might have held toward yourself.

Declare to yourself something like this:

I have cleansed my heart and mind of all feelings of guilt. I have made mistakes and have profited by them. I face the future with a sense of self-appreciation because I know I have everything I need to build a long life of profound happiness, which I shall do.

Repeat this statement just before retiring every evening until you find that all feeling of guilt has disappeared.

All chapters in this book are of great importance. This one is particularly so.

CHAPTER 5

The Love for Life

A genuine love for life can be positive or negative, so far as it applies to one's age.

One can become so devoted to life that he will dread its coming to an end, and can, thereby, develop an age-consciousness. And, as we are learning, a consciousness of age will hasten age.

Developing the type of interest in life that causes us to look to the future for a continuation of life's blessings, instead of wincing each time we think of the present ebbing into the past, will help one to develop a long-life consciousness.

Robert Oram once told me that he had reached the time in life where he was becoming bored with it all. He had been an avid reader and he had traveled much. He felt he knew all about life. Although he was not contemplating suicide, he was impatiently waiting for the end. Naturally such an attitude was causing him to grow old physically much earlier than Nature had intended.

One day, he fell heir to an assortment of personal effects which had belonged to a brother who had passed away. Among these items was a fine microscope. One afternoon, just to pass time, Oram played with his new "toy." The first thing he did was to take a hair from his own head and look at it through the powerful microscope. What he saw amazed him. The hair was enlarged to the point where it appeared as big around as a pencil, and he could view the surface of the hair just as he could the bark on a tree, —and even see the texture of the surface.

He took a small leaf from a plant. The enlargement brought out the veins of the leaf in full view. It gave him a new concept of the perfection of Nature.

An aquarium was in the room and a green scum, known as algae, had begun to form on the inside of the glass. Oram rubbed his finger on the glass and placed a bit of the algae under the microscope. Instead of appearing as unsightly scum, it, when greatly magnified, became a most interesting form of plant life.

It wasn't long before Robert Oram realized that, instead of knowing too much about life, he knew practically nothing. With his new viewpoint, he lost his feeling of boredom, and, upon arising in the morning, he looked forward to a new and exciting day.

To love life means to fully become aware as to what life really is. Let us begin with the human body.

Nothing on the face of the earth can compare to the wonders contained within that body of yours.

It took science many years to develop the camera, an instrument which "sees" an object and then registers it on a film. It took many more years to reproduce objects, things and people in motion— motion pictures.

Not a ray of light ever enters the brain. Yet the human eyes can project into the brain every lighted object or person, in full color and motion.

One feels rather smart if he lives in an air-conditioned home. Have you ever thought of Nature's air-conditioning plant contained within every human body? Regardless of the external temperature— whether hot or cold—the blood temperature remains the same.

In our modern laboratories, science has taught men how to take an item and break it down into its component parts and to remove desired elements from the object.

Within your being is a laboratory capable of doing things not possible in any man-made laboratory in existence. From the food you eat, elements necessary for blood, bone, tissue, energy, etc., are constantly being extracted without any conscious thought whatsoever.

Can you imagine automobile tires repairing themselves as they become damaged or wear down?

Think of your own body. Nature is constantly replacing tissue and, if you should cut yourself, Nature begins at once to restore the flesh and skin to their original condition.

Take some time and reflect over the wonders of that body which you possess. You will reach a point where you will realize that, if you didn't have a material thing on earth, you are still wealthy, merely by owning a replica of God's greatest handiwork.

"Why does this marvelous body grow old?" might come as your big question. And, it is a sound, logical question. One cannot stop it from growing old from the calendar standpoint, but through the right mental attitude, the physiological aging processes can definitely be retarded. But, remember, pages back you promised me that you would live as though your life would go on forever.

Right now we are learning how to really love life. We are beginning by gaining an enthusiastic appreciation for the body—and a few of its many wonders.

Love life! Do the birds provide you with enjoyment? In my patio is a bird feeding station—which is kept filled with wild-bird seed, pieces of suet, bread crumbs and once in a while fine cut corn. Adjacent to this is a bird bath, always containing clean, fresh water. The large window in our breakfast room overlooks this area which has become a sanctuary for birds of all kinds. Although we have not become "bird watchers" to the extent that the study of them has become an obsession, or even a hobby, they do bring much happiness into our lives. We have gotten to know our feathered friends. We have learned how to distinguish birds of various kinds, and have found interest in learning the characteristics of each. For example, we find that, although most birds move by hopping, there are species which walk, such as the blackbirds and quail.

Loving all forms of animal life—wild and domestic—will put something fine into your life.

Every now and then, I like to find time to spend a few hours at a zoo. You can find something to like about all of the creatures housed there; the brilliant colors of the feathers of the birds and fowl; the fur on many of the animals, and the human-like behavior of members of the ape family.

How about the plant life? Once you get yourself in rhythm with Nature, you'll find something to like about all plant life—from the tiny blades of grass up to the giant trees. And flowers of all kinds will never cease to be a wonder to you.

Sunrises and sunsets will forever run a tingle up your spine as you see a master blending of color which might be imitated by man, but never duplicated.

Love Life! So far we have considered our own physical beings; animal and plant life. Now—let us think of all humanity. And, everything I will say about people can be summed up in two words: Like People!

Shakespeare referred to the world as a great stage and the people the actors. This, of course, is an interesting observation, but I like to think of the world as a great mirror. It reflects to us exactly what we project into it.

It we like people, people will like us. Do you know that what you consciously see in others is a reflection of what you subconsciously have within?

Some years ago I discovered what I have found to be the keynote of personal magnetism. This discovery not only helped me but, through my teaching and writing, has been of immeasurable help to countless thousands of others. I have always been an advocate of the theory: To have people like you, you must like people. This is true, of course, but there is one person in particular you must like and that is—as I said in an earlier chapter—yourself. Sounds egotistical, perhaps, but it is not. My own experience will make this point clear.

In my younger days I did not have too much respect for myself. In fact, I often felt that I actually hated the reflection which projected itself to me each time I looked into the mirror. This was during the days I did some drinking. No, I was not a drunkard, but I consumed more of the alcoholic beverages than I should; and, I also smoked quite heavily.

The weekend was over, but the memory lingered on. Perhaps the memory was a bit too vivid for comfort. I sat on the edge of the bed, dressing slowly. It was Monday morning and I kept avoiding a direct gaze into the mirror in front of me. My headache was the for-get-me-not that kept the holiday activities alive in my mind.

No, I hadn't dissipated too much. My wife was away and, to keep from being lonely, I did invite the boys over on Saturday night for a friendly game; and those who did not fare too well insisted we do the same thing Sunday night to give them a chance to retrieve their chips. And, when one does with too little sleep, he "pays the price."

As I sat there feeling sorry for myself, the phone rang. It was a long-distance call from my wife—not trying to check up on me, because she never did that—she merely wanted to hear my voice at the start of the week, and to tell me she loved me.

Returning to the bedside to finish tying the strings of my shoes, I caught another glimpse of the man I definitely hated—myself.

"It's a lucky thing my wife has a better opinion of me than I have," I thought. For some strange and fortunate reason, that thought led to others, and soon I found myself engulfed in a myriad of questions.

"My wife loves me, why can't I like myself?"

"I am still able to make a fairly good living, should not that give me a good opinion of myself?"

"My neighbors all seem to respect me, why can't I respect my-self?"

And on and on it went—one question after another, until I reached the jackpot question: "If I can get by and have people like me—when I do not like myself—how much more progress could I make if I should develop genuine self-appreciation?" This question was challenging to such an extent, I lingered over my coffee for a seemingly long time, meditating over it.

"Why don't I like myself?" This question kept returning, though I tried to evade it. Sized up with other men, I fared well. Although not in the big money, I was not doing badly. My credit standing was all right. I had no more than the usual number of bad habits. For a while, there seemed to be no answer to the question haunting me. WHY? WHY? WHY?

I must have been born not with a silver spoon in my mouth, but with a question mark over my head. "Why, why, why?" I am constantly asking regarding almost everything. This three-letter word came to the fore in connection with my antipathy toward myself. The only answer which appeared at all satisfying was that I was a perfectionist and, knowing everything I was doing, and am capable of doing, I hold myself accountable for the fact that I am not doing my best.

Those words "I love you" previously given over the phone by my wife kept ringing in my ears. And perhaps it was these three words which caused me to take steps in the right direction.

My wife knows me quite well, I reasoned. She knows my weaknesses as well as my strength—and with this knowledge—she loves me. "Why can't I accept myself as I am and really like myself?" I queried.

"I Have It!"

Have you ever watched a puzzled man on the screen, as he stares off into space; he suddenly will snap his fingers and enthusiastically proclaim: "I have it!" Well, that is how I felt. I had suddenly realized why I was not making greater headway in life, and how easily I could change my circumstances.

Not that I intend delving into magic; but my mind did revert to an exhibition I had witnessed at my club one evening when a magician held us spellbound with his feats of legerdemain. With perfect poise and confidence he performed one trick after another which seemed incredible. In reflecting over the dexterity of this Knight of the Wand, I realized that one must develop self-appreciation to a marked degree in order to manifest such skill.

I thought of the surgeon whose infinite skill had saved my wife's life after she had been in a bad automobile accident. Could such unerring precision be produced by a man who didn't like himself?

Then, there was Toni, the boot black. I often let him shine my shoes just to watch the pride he takes in his work. After applying the polish, he beats a rhythmic tattoo on my shoes with his cloth, then steps back and admiringly surveys his deft touch to the leather. That man could not possibly dislike himself, and take such an interest in his work, I reasoned.

"Why Can't I Like Myself?"

My thoughts returned to my original question: "Why can't I like myself?" In meditating over this interrogation, a parade of minor infractions passed before my mental gaze. I recalled many things, dating back to school days, things I had done, which were not altogether right. Even now I could think of things I should be doing that I had been neglecting; and, too, I could think of things I am doing, which should not be done.

Wasn't it Elbert Hubbard who said: "Love a man for his virtues and be tolerant of his faults"? Why couldn't this thought apply to one's opinion of himself? Why couldn't he develop self-appreciation for his constructive characteristics, and cease focusing too much attention on his negative qualities?

The Prospector Reaches "Pay-Dirt!"

I felt like a prospector who had just reached pay-dirt, Already I was beginning to feel friendlier toward myself. If I am fond of people who have as many, if not more, faults than I have, then why shouldn't I, under the same circumstances, like myself?

With this entirely new line of reasoning, I no longer shied from my mirror reflection. In fact, I stepped quite close to it and carefully examined myself, and to my pleasant surprise, found a new me casting a friendly glance into my eyes.

Had Everything I Needed

Endophasia is the name psychiatrists use when they refer to one talking to himself. Well, right then and there I became a victim of endophasia. I talked to myself in dead earnest. I realized I had everything I needed in order to make a success, and was going to be a success. "What are we waiting for?" I asked, referring to my reflection as a twin. There was no reason for further delay. I turned and rushed eagerly to the room I call my den.

My Daily Reminder

Slipping a sheet of paper into my typewriter, I wrote: "I like myself, and I will do everything I can to justify the self-respect." I trimmed the sheet neatly and with a bit of adhesive tape, fastened it to the inside of my closet where it would act as a reminder each time I went for my coat and hat.

I did expect to make more money as a result of my changed attitude toward myself—and I did. My business mounted steadily and substantially. Naturally, the added income was welcome, because it enabled me to do more for my wife and to start a nest egg which would provide a sense of security for the future.

Money Not Everything!

Strangely enough, the extra money was not my greatest reward. Things started to happen, lots of them, all contributing to a richer and fuller life.

"Ben, you seem to grow finer and sweeter day by day," my wife affectionately commented, then added: "Your disposition is far better than it was. Not that I had any difficulty in living with you as you were, but now you wake up with a smile on your lips, which makes my day so happy."

Elected to Office

One noon, at my luncheon club, the president surprised me by saying: "Will you become chairman of the Membership Committee? You have such a magnetic personality, you will find it easy to persuade others to join the club."

Probably the incident which made the greatest impression on me was when a small neighborhood urchin unexpectedly said: "Mister, you're just about the finest man on this block." And, think of it, prior to becoming friendly with myself, I never paid the slightest notice to children. If they tried to get my attention, I would ignore them.

The World Is a Mirror

The world is a mirror that reflects to us that which we project into it.

To be liked by others, we must like ourselves. Expressing the same thought in other words, one might say: The opinions others have of us is no different than the opinion we have of ourselves.

There is a story taken from my file of case histories that will make a fitting conclusion to this chapter:

An employer asked me if I would take a special interest in one of the men in his sales department. "This man is quickly going to the dogs," the executive confided. "I'm not only thinking of him, but of his family which is suffering due to him."

This salesman had been getting business under false pretenses and was not as honest as he might be in handling his firm's money, yet, through sympathy, the man at the head of the company, instead of discharging him, wanted to try, if possible, to rehabilitate him.

The chap came to my office and, while talking, could not look me in the eye. His gaze shifted from the ceiling to the floor.

Why did this man dread looking at me? Was he afraid of me? No, he did not like himself and was uncomfortable when another was looking at the one he greatly disliked.

My caller had no respect for himself and instinctively felt others could not respect him.

For nearly an hour I talked to this miserable man about developing self-appreciation. He could not change his past, but he could profit by it.

A month later this man dropped into my office and the transformation was hard to believe. He was an entirely different man in every respect. With perfect poise—and the ability to look me squarely in the eye as he talked—he related what had been happening to him since his former visit. He had greatly increased his earnings and was being promoted to assistant sales manager.

"Ben, people like me, because I am now living in a manner which permits me to like myself," were his parting words as he left my office.

Summary

Love Life! To love life and everything which pertains to it is to give you a major incentive for wanting to regain youth and add years to your life.

Learn to appreciate yourself. We are often our own worst critics. Develop an appreciation for your good qualities. Take time each week to reflect on your accomplishments and good deeds.

To increase your self-esteem, do things worthy of esteem. Become a person who deserves respect.

Motion creates emotion. Before starting on the next chapter, reflect over this one. Determine now that from this moment onward you will find something to like about everybody and everything.

Life will take on a new radiance as you find yourself feeling younger—and far happier.

CHAPTER 6

Mental Pictures and Patterns

Human beings have two means of seeing. We see through our physical eyes and we see through our mind's eye.

The physical eyes, if normal, are capable of seeing all which lies before them, within a reasonable distance. If, in a room, one can see every exposed item in that room. He may step outside, and by moving his head and body, see great distances in all directions. Everything he sees must be in direct line of his vision. He cannot see behind objects; he cannot see beneath the ground.

The mind's eye is virtually unlimited as to what it can see. It can bring into consciousness everything ever seen by the physical eyes, which has been retained in the memory. It can translate into mental pictures everything read or heard. And, through imagination, can see things which do not exist.

The mind's eye is capable of "seeing" thousands of times more than the physical eyes. We pity the sightless person, yet the portion of sight he has lost is infinitesimal compared to the ability to mentally "see," which he retains.

The physical eyes, of course, are highly desirable. They not only guide us as to our movements, but enable us to store impressions of people and things as they are. Without ever having had physical eyesight, the impression one gains of objects and people is based upon the remaining four of the five senses; hearing, taste, smell and touch.

While such mental impressions might suffice, they usually differ greatly from reality.

Mental Pictures Influence One's Health and Well-Being

To say that we are affected, physically, by the mental pictures we hold might indicate I am about to indulge in some -ism, cult or dogma. I am not! Permit me to give a few illustrations.

When you think of your "old home town," how do you picture the people you formerly knew? Do you see them as they are today, or as they were many years ago? We are shocked when we visit our old home. The vivacious redhead of school days is now a gray-haired grandma. That athletic young man who won all the running and jumping contests in school, now limps along on his cane.

Do you know that people who lose their sight in their early days, stay young longer than those with sight? Do you know why? Just as we retain pictures of our former school mates as they were when we last saw them, so, too, do blind people retain the picture of themselves as they last saw their reflections.

With our physical eyes, we become accustomed to seeing people as they look when in the 60's, 70's, 80's and beyond.

As we reach the older brackets, we begin seeing ourselves as we think we should look based upon what we see in others of like age.

This means that when we reach 50, for instance, we see ourselves as we should look at 50, so our mental pictures are accepted as patterns and we begin to show our age. In other words, we have established a mental pattern on which our subconscious minds work. When we go to the mirror, we do not look for signs of youth, we examine our foreheads for age wrinkles; around the corners of our eyes for "crow's feet"; our necks for sagginess. Lines which might be on the face, due to the serious expression we have, are accentuated. So, we leave the mirror feeling certain we are "showing our age." Of course, the mental pictures we have of ourselves as growing old puts the forces of Nature to work in accelerating the aging processes.

If you can make yourself young in mind, it will reflect in your body. As simple as this sounds, it is not easy. We try to do this, and, for a time, we believe we have succeeded. Later, we find nothing is happening and we lose courage to try further. We often find that instead of becoming younger, we might go the other way and suddenly grow older.

This does not mean that sometimes the principle works and sometimes it does not. The difficulty is that instead of actually seeing yourself as young, you are in reality, wishing to be young.

Wishing for youth indicates you haven't got it, nor do you expect to get it, otherwise you would not wish for it. This makes sense, doesn't it?

Digestion and Health

Not everyone knows the part mental pictures play in digestion.

We chew our food, not only to reduce it in size so that we can swallow it without choking, but to mix with it the first digestive juice, the saliva. Digestion actually starts in the mouth.

The flow of this digestive juice is psychological as well as physiological.

When meal time comes and you see the food you like which carries with it a tempting aroma, your mouth begins to water. Your glands accelerate the flow of the digestive juice. This is Nature preparing you for proper digestion. You see, it is the thought, sight and smell of the food which increased the flow of the essential saliva.

Suppose, for example, you are very hungry and are about to enjoy a delicious meal; suddenly you get some bad news! Your appetite leaves you and the flow of digestive juice drops to normal. Now then, should you eat under such circumstances, your food would not digest properly because it was not prepared with a sufficient amount of saliva.

Right now, as an experiment, close your eyes and begin visualizing the item of food you like extremely well. It might be a thick steak, sizzling in the broiler, the juice oozing and the tantalizing scent wafting through the kitchen. What happens? Your mouth begins to water. This is psychological—not physiological. It was thought—mental pictures—that started the flow of the important digestive Juice.

Suppose you were eating an apple and should be told you had eaten a worm—you hadn't of course—you were merely told you had. You would become ill, wouldn't you? You might even vomit. You would suffer all of this physical distress through no other cause than mental pictures.

Is Fatigue Psychosomatic?

Fatigue results most frequently from mental pictures.

One becomes tired because he expects to get tired. Early in the morning, before the day starts, a person will often review the work ahead of him, and actually start the day tired—in anticipation of the work.

Little Johnny quickly tires when he is called upon to do some of the household chores. Notice how much energy he will expend when doing something he enjoys doing— swimming, for instance; and without any sign of fatigue.

A man arrives home after a day's work at the office and is dog tired. His day's work consisted of sitting at his desk, talking on the telephone and dictating a few letters. But, he will go to the country club and play 18, or more, holes of golf and arrive home commenting on how good an afternoon of golf makes him feel; notwithstanding the fact he uses far more energy than he does spending a full day at his office.

"How do you stand such a busy schedule?" many ask me; those who know the large number of crowded hours I put in every day. "It would kill me," they say.

"I like my work, and make it my avocation as well as vocation," I tell them.

A man will laboriously work for several hours at a time in his hobby shop, and claim the work is relaxing and actually energizing. The same amount of time spent in doing things he is supposed to do will bring on a condition of marked fatigue.

With fatigue is associated self-pity. The one who is constantly tired usually pities himself.

The one who pities himself will create a chain of mental pictures whereby he sees himself tired because he is constantly under such a strain.

Can't you see what happens? He begins to picture himself as being not as "young as he used to be." He imagines himself as growing old. He sees himself taking on the characteristics of old age. And, as we are learning, the mental pictures we hold are accepted by the subconscious mind which reproduces them in our beings. We do accelerate age—both in feelings and in looks.

Become a Picture Editor

Pictures play a highly important part in many of the national magazines. Of the thousands of pictures constantly being submitted, only a small fraction of them are used. The picture editor selects only the pictures which will build circulation.

Knowing the potency of mental pictures, you should think of yourself as a picture editor, knowing that some pictures are beneficial—others detrimental. Each time a negative picture—one bearing on old age, for instance, tempts to enter your mind, delete it. Cast it aside. Remember, the more you encourage positive mental pictures the more you will automatically eliminate the negative ones.

Pattern for Mental Discipline

You will now be given a routine to follow which will help you to develop the type of a mind which refuses the entrance of destructive old age thoughts. Follow it faithfully according to the prescribed outline. You will be astonished to find that you are actually turning back the hands of the clock of time.

1. Become youth conscious. Build on the thought: "I am young." Every time you think of it, repeat to yourself: "I am young."

At first it might seem like you are trying to fool yourself, but no matter. Keep on keeping on. Say it—think it: "I am young!"

Are you a doodler? When talking on the phone, are you using your pencil in making all sorts of meaningless designs? If so, good! But, instead of drawing designs, write: "I am young!" Write it many times, in many ways. You might print it, you might use ordinary handwriting. You see? You are putting your doodling to work for you.

2. When seeing others who might be showing their age, instead of letting it impress itself on your mind—be happy in the thought that you are actually getting younger.

To create and possess youth, we must maintain mental pictures of youth. At this point it might be well to reach an understanding as to what we mean when we say youth. In referring to youth, I mean that state of being where you actually feel young, where you can enjoy the activities of youth, when your face shows that glad-to-be-alive sparkle of youth, and your mind is active and alert. This is our objective regarding youth.

3. Become youthful in action. Do the things you did in your younger days. Did you enjoy dancing? It so, dance now. Did you like to swim? Do the same now, whenever possible. Acting young is a sure way to develop mental pictures of youth.

If you are suffering from any physical condition which might make it unwise to indulge in any activity calling for the use of energy, it is advised that you first consult your physician for his sanction.

4. Dress young. A friend of mine, a man in the late 40's, always dressed very conservatively. He wore gray suits, white shirts and gray or black ties, black socks and black shoes. He looked like an elderly man just waiting for his day of earthly departure to come.

I induced this man to buy a suit with a little life to it.

He should wear a colorful tie, and socks which displayed more than the shape and size of his ankle.

There was an immediate change in my friend's personality. He looked years younger. There was expression in his voice instead of the halt one notices in the voice of age.

The listless look in his eyes had gone and was replaced with a gleam which reflected an alert mind. And, it was interesting to detect a more sprightly spring in his step.

To suggest that you dress young does not mean to be gaudy in your dress.

Men and women in the so-called middle life or beyond should not dress like college boys or debutantes. However they can wear colorful clothes and still be in good taste.

A picture should be framed so that the frame will blend with the picture; so that you will not see a picture and a frame, but a harmonious whole.

An individual should be dressed so that you will not feel you are looking at a man and a suit, but the complete ensemble.

5. Be happy! Have you ever noticed how much older a person looks when he is unhappy? Looking old, however, is not the only negative reaction to gloom. An unhappy person—or one with a bad disposition, is always complaining of aches and pains.

Gloom and anger interfere with all bodily functions. Digestion is impaired, and poor digestion can cause many different types of ailments: intestinal sluggishness, headaches, etc.

Unhappiness is negative. One with a sad mind will see the black side of every situation. He thinks of himself as being old and growing older. He has no feeling of security.

It is impossible to overemphasize the potency of the admonition: Be Happy! You might adopt every suggestion so far given in this book, and not get the results you have a right to expect, if you keep your mind in an unhappy state.

"How can I be happy when I have to contend with so-and-so and such-and-such?" you might ask.

Everyone has to contend with many things that could prove unpleasant. Some people master circumstances, other people will permit circumstances to master them.

It might be well to understand what happiness really is. It is not something you obtain—and put on—as you do clothes—or cosmetics. Happiness is an emotion which one expresses. A whole chapter is being devoted to happiness and will explain in considerable detail how to give expression to the happiness which you now have within. But, before even reaching that chapter, begin now in doing everything you can to develop a happy mind. It will help you to make immediate use of everything you have learned so far.

Begin Developing Your Mental Pictures

When an artist prepares to make a painting, he mounts his canvas, then places it on his easel. Before applying his brush, he may spend a few moments staring at the canvas. What does he see? Is his gaze focused on the woof and weft of the cloth? No, he does not even see the threads making up the material. He sees on the canvas the picture which he has created in his mind's eye; a picture which will soon become a part of the canvas.

Beginning today, start seeing, in your mind's eye, yourself as you desire to be. See yourself with a face of glowing health. Think of your mind as being active and alert. See your body alive and vigorous.

"How can I see these things in my imagination when my physical eyes see the opposite?" you might ask. In answering this question, I might use a sculptor as an illustration.

When a sculptor begins a project, he starts out with a rough, jagged stone. The picture of reality his physical eyes observe do not make him discouraged. Not a bit! As he looks at the stone, his mind's eye sees the completed bust or statue.

With what you have read so far, you should understand that as you visualize (which means to create mental pictures) yourself as being younger and more active, you are actually giving your subconscious mind a pattern to follow in making your mental pictures a reality.

Do Not Watch for Results

It might seem quite contradictory for me to say at this time that you should not watch for results. I have been telling you how much you will benefit by the thoughts being given, now I tell you not to watch for results. There is a most logical reason.

You can't see a plant grow. Should you sit by it watching, you would soon come to the conclusion that nothing was happening. But, if you leave the plant alone for a few days, then examine it, you will be surprised as to how much it has grown.

If you keep running to your mirror every hour to see what changes have taken place, you'll see no change because it has been so slight. But, if you carry on knowing that your new type of thinking is taking root, it will not be long until your friends will be asking what has happened, you seem so much younger. You will begin noticing how much more energy you have, how much more you are enjoying life.

Summary

In this chapter I have attempted to prove to you that "You Are What You Think You Are!"

The mental pictures you hold are patterns which are accepted by the subconscious mind which proceeds to reproduce them in your being.

Create new mental pictures with your actions. Choose an activity you enjoy that you have not done in years and do it! Wear something colorful. Create your new self-image as an active, youthful person.

This chapter is an important one. Do not treat it lightly. If, at this very moment, you are not excitedly enthusiastic, you have not read the chapter thoughtfully enough. You have not concentrated on what you have been reading. If this does apply to you, please re-read it before proceeding to Chapter Seven.

CHAPTER 7

Sex As It Applies to Age

The sexes were made for each other, and only in the wise and loving union of the two is the fullness of health and duty and happiness to be expected. ---
W. HALL

There are probably few things which add to one's age consciousness more than to feel his sexual powers are on the wane. Since this condition is more psychological than physiological, it is quite fitting that the subject of sex be given consideration in this book.

Although the chapter is written mainly from the standpoint of husbands and wives, others will be interested in the thinking on this most important subject.

When just a boy, I heard some of the older children talking about something new to me. They were using the word "womb" and I could tell by the expression on their faces that it was taboo, at least so far as children are concerned. Being a child with a large bump of curiosity, I wanted to learn more about the subject, so at dinner when family was together, I blurted out: "Ma, what is a womb?" Mother, being a New England Puritanical type woman, blushed deeply and warned me not to associate with anyone who used such language. I did not learn the meaning of the word—at the time.

The act responsible for pregnancy was never discussed by refined people, and for a child to even know of the existence of such an act was a sin beyond all reasonable comprehension.

Expectant mothers would conceal their predicament as much as possible, and those in the know would whisper in a hush-hush fashion: "Mary is going to have a baby."

Much progress has been made toward bringing sex out in the open where it belongs, and as a greater understanding of the subject is gained, men and women will find more happiness and success in life.

In the little consultation work for which I have found time, at least one out of every three problems presented has had a bearing on sex. Husbands would tell of their frigid wives. Wives would bemoan the fact that their husbands were inconsiderate, at least so far as the intimate relation is concerned. Then I would hear from wives who would tell of the impotency of their husbands; and even husbands would ask me if there is anything they can do to correct or avoid it. Although this discussion cannot be considered as a treatise on the subject of sex, I do believe that from my study and observations, I can add a few thoughts on the subject which will be of value to all wives and husbands.

I am approaching this topic from the standpoint of Godliness of Sex; not lust or mere physical gratification. Children are taught the stories of the bees; they learn with eager eyes of the mother birds with their varicolored eggs; the stories of flowers and seeds are a part of their early education. Then, why should we arch an eyebrow when a subject which pertains to human reproduction is discussed? This is a logical question.

Three Phases to a Happy Marriage

There are three phases to marriage as I see it: Spiritual, Mental and Physical. Like the three-legged stool which will fall if a leg is removed, so, too, will marriage fail if one or more of these essentials are not properly considered. Not all such marriages will end in divorce, but they will not be happy marriages. Books could be written on Spiritual and Mental incompatibility, but we are considering only a third of the marital triangle: Physical, or sex.

So that you may determine in advance whether or not you wish to continue reading this chapter, I would like to declare my feelings toward the intimate side of marriage.

I believe that a couple should be harmonious sexually as well as temperamentally.

I believe that the sex relations between husband and wife should, and can be, maintained on a level of beauty and looked upon as being wholesome and clean and, yes, even divine.

I do not believe it is natural to become impotent at so-called middle-age, as is so generally accepted.

I believe that in a majority of cases impotency is more psychological than physiological, and can be corrected through a change of mental attitude.

I believe that sexual powers can be retained over a longer period of years through proper use than through abstinence.

I believe that just as the trees and plants begin to die after they have stopped reproducing themselves, so too, do humans begin to show advanced age as they cease intimate relations.

I DO NOT believe in sexual promiscuity.

Formula for Marital Happiness

Shortly after entering the field of radio, one of my listeners asked me for a formula a couple should use in assuring marital happiness. I suggested that if the husband would forget self and do everything within his power to make his wife happy; and if the wife would likewise forget self and do everything within her power to make her husband happy, only happiness could result. There would be no discord. This same thought could be advanced so far as the sex act is concerned. If the husband would concentrate his thoughts— entirely—on the pleasure he could extend to his wife, and the wife would take the same attitude, can't you see how harmonious this phase of marriage could be? There is only one answer.

The mistake made by most husbands and wives regarding sex, is considering that the climax—the orgasm—is the objective. Through a concentration on this objective it is reached far too hastily; frequently before one of the union is properly prepared, with the result that the husband or wife is "cheated." Usually at dinner, the dessert is the tastiest part of the meal; but we do not eat a meal merely to enjoy the dessert. If time permits, we linger over the entire dinner, making it as long and as enjoyable as possible.

Marital intimacies should really be nocturnal banquets. Both parties should be freshly bathed; the breath sweet and the husband tree from facial stubble. The close contact; the caressing; that indescribable reflection of harmonious love; all should create such heavenly ecstasy that the "dessert"—the climax—would be delayed as long as possible, instead of being hastened.

What I am saying might seem like idealizing instead of facing facts as they exist, and, perhaps, that would be the most helpful thing for me to do. While there are many complaints on the part of husbands as to the marital relations, I have found, and believe, there are more legitimate causes for complaint on the part of wives. The most common one is that the husband is inconsiderate; thinking only of himself. He expects the wife to be ready anytime he is and after the contact is made, the husband concludes long before his wife has even had a chance to build up a normal desire. This condition, I feel, is frequently true, and, perhaps, a correction can be made resulting in greater marriage happiness.

"Getting ready" for a man is purely a mental condition. Within the male organ are several hollow cavities which are normally empty. In the vein which carries blood from the organ is a valve which is usually open, permitting the free flow of blood. Through emotional excitement, this valve closes sufficiently to cause the blood to back up, filling the hollow cavities causing a state of rigidity. After the excitement is over, the valve opens, permitting the blood to leave the cavities, restoring the organ to its original relaxed state.

In the early days of marriage, the sex act is frequently indulged in to such an extent that the glamor is lost. The couple takes each other for granted and the intimate relation which could mean so much in keeping romance alive, becomes routine affair. Under such conditions, it is not too easy for the husband to function as he did during the honeymoon days. He manages to get himself in condition, but knows that unless he can retain his emotional excitement, he will "lose it," so he hastens to make a physical contact with his mate, before she has had an opportunity of developing the proper mood, and so that he can complete the operation before he loses what he has, he focuses his attention on the climax rather than on the pleasure he might otherwise be giving his mate.

Impotency Not an Indication of Age

A common cause of psychological impotency on the part of the male, is criticism from his wife. Accusing him of "not being the man he should be" brings on a type of timidity which makes it difficult for the man to properly function. He might succeed in getting partially ready when fear of criticism will enter his mind and cause him to lose all feeling for the relation.

Impotency on the part of the husband is not always an indication of age. Frequently men in the 20's and 30's will reach a state where they have great difficulty in functioning as a husband. On the other hand, there is no reason why men of normal physical condition and with the right attitude toward sex should not remain sexually active until they reach the 70's and beyond.

A case came to my attention where a woman divorced her husband because he was impotent. She was 38, he was 42. During the last few years of their marriage, months would elapse between any sexual union. The husband told me that he really felt he was "on the shelf." But, about three years later this man met and married an understanding young lady. To this wife he is proving to be a most virile, lover-type husband. And, bear in mind, he was several years older than he was when the first wife branded him impotent. The "technique" used by this second wife, according to what the husband told me, was interesting indeed. The wife proved not only to be a good wife, but a real psychologist as well. After retiring, they would snuggle up to each other, and she would suggest that he take his time about "getting ready," the longer the better. It is easy to understand that under such conditions there would be no nervous tension on his part and that nature really would take its course.

If I were to sum up in a single sentence all I have given so far, I would say: The Marital Congress should be an act of love and never a routine part of "family duty." It should be based on a mutual desire to give happiness rather than to receive it. This being true, the relation should be kept on an extremely high plane. Make a ceremony of it, if you please, knowing that the more you put into the act, the greater will be your reward.

Too Old for Sex?

Too old for sex? Nonsense! It is my personal belief that one ages more rapidly through the absence of sex relations than otherwise. Nothing stands still; it either goes forward or backward. When a tree or plant stops reproducing itself, it is all through. Husbands and wives who slow down in their intimacies are beckoning to Father Time to hasten with his scythe.

Why do couples slow down in this regard? Because they have allowed the relation to become commonplace.

On a trip I was visited by a sweet young lady who was in her early 60's. She consulted me regarding her daughter and son-in-law who were not getting along too well, and the difficulty was largely due to sexual incompatibility. This mother told me of her own marital bliss and blushed like a bride when she told me that her husband, then 72, was still virile and a real lover. I am quite well acquainted with a man of 84, whose sex life is still normal. He looks far younger than most men of his years and possesses an alertness not always found in men his age.

How About Promiscuity?

Let's talk a bit about promiscuity. It is certain that many divorces result from infidelity; either the husband or wife having affairs away from home. What causes this? Why do men seek a change? Why do women give in to temptation? There is always one basic answer. One seeks something he does not already possess. I am certain I am right when I say that the thought of divorce seldom enters the home where there is a harmonious understanding regarding sex.

I hope that what I have said up to this point does not indicate that I imply sex to be the big issue in marriage. It is not by any means. I have attempted to point out in my humble way that the institution of marriage will be on a sounder foundation when there is a proper understanding of the responsibility of mate to mate so far as sex is concerned.

It is my belief that children should receive sex information early in life and should be impressed with the purity of the act, rather than otherwise. They will endeavor to retain it on its high plane if proper judgment is used by the parents in imparting the information. Instead of trying to frighten the children regarding the loss of virginity, create the desire within them to remain virgins and be able to bring into marriage one of our great God given treasures.

The Three Fundamentals

You were told early in this chapter that a successful marriage is based on three fundamentals; Spiritual, Mental and Physical. I have advanced a few thoughts on one phase only. Libraries contain countless books on sex, and in this modern age, newspapers and magazines are carrying sex articles which would have been banned not long ago. This wide dissemination of information on the subject, to my mind, is a distinct evidence of progress.

Before bringing this subject to a close, however, I wish to leave just a thought regarding the other two phases of marital happiness. Remember what I said to the effect that to remove any one of the three would weaken the structure of marriage. If your attraction to each other is sex alone, regardless how well you might be mated in that direction, you will soon reach a point of sexual boredom and might seek other pastures. But, if you are spiritually and mentally compatible and love each other for the mind and soul you have, you will find your sex life, too, will be kept more actively alive.

If your married life is not all you dreamed of during the courting days, instead of permitting the marital ship to rock, perhaps to the point of capsizing, why not study your marriage; study it from all three angles, the Spiritual, the Mental and the Physical, and see if you cannot discover any weaknesses which have been existing so that they might be corrected.

And, remember! Making a success of your marriage is proving your leadership in directing one of the greatest institutions on the face of the earth.

Summary

Life is a continuous cycle: birth, reproduction, death. It seems reasonable to assume, therefore, that when the reproduction powers cease to function, birth is stopped, and one heads rapidly toward the third phase, death.

Keeping the second phase of life alive and active, enhances the possibilities of birth and greatly extends one's life.

Develop a new appreciation for your partner.

Since we have just been talking about a subject closely related to birth, I will continue in the next chapter with a consideration of death, and how to overcome the fear of it.

CHAPTER **8**

Overcoming the Fear of Death

Cowards die many times before their deaths; the valiant never taste of death but once.—SHAKESPEARE

The fear of death hastens death. In this chapter the truth of this statement will be proved. You will learn why we fear death, and how easy it is to prolong our lives through the elimination of the fear of death.

"A fault discovered is half overcome," is an aphorism quite well known. In the same vein we might say: "It we know the reason for a fault, it will be much easier to overcome."

There is a reason—sometimes several reasons—why one fears death. Let us examine some of these reasons to see if they apply to us; and, if they do, find out what we can do to correct the cause and change the effect.

Fear of the Unknown. Most of us, from childhood up have drilled into us that we are sinners, and that "sin must pay the price." People with such beliefs fear death because they are afraid their souls will be submitted to eternal torment.

As I covered in an earlier chapter, none of us can relive the past, but we can profit by it. If we will do everything we can to live honorably in the future, following, let us say—the Golden Rule—it is my firm belief we need not fear what will happen to us after we pass from this plane of existence.

Guilty Conscience is closely allied to the fear we have for the unknown. Those who have knowingly committed sins, and who have become confused—because of the conflicting thoughts regarding life beyond—will most likely fear death.

Many people have an instinctive fear of darkness. When they think of death, they imagine the horror of being locked in a casket and buried in a deep, dark hole—many feet below the surface of the ground.

The thought of cremation causes many people to cringe as they imagine their own bodies being reduced to ashes under intense heat.

Family responsibilities are probably the cause of most fears of death. If a man's estate is involved with many obligations, the considerate one will dread death because of the hardships his demise would leave with those who survive him. This, of course, can be avoided if we strive at all times to keep our affairs in such shape that should we pass on, those we leave behind can carry on without difficulties. There is a caution to be observed in this connection, however. By having our affairs in good shape, we should not become complacent, and literally give up.

A man of my acquaintance—he was close to 70—told me that since he was reaching old age, he wanted to get his estate so arranged that when he died his wife and children would have no problems in taking over. After he had gathered in all the loose ends, he remarked that he could now go with a clear conscience. Without any more feeling that he was needed and that his job here was completed, he passed away.

Have you ever noticed how comparatively few people there are who die while they travel? Even though their physical conditions might indicate their stay on this earth is coming to an end, when they are on trips they remain alive and active until after their return. Why is this? Subconsciously they know they should return and their subconscious minds build up enough energy to allow them to complete their missions. This illustration, of course, does not take into consideration deaths resulting from accidents; most of which are caused by conditions beyond our control.

Business responsibilities, to the conscientious man, can easily cause a fear of death. Attaining predetermined objectives may make him want to live until after completion. And, as I already stated earlier, the fear of death can hasten it.

Relinquishing possessions will cause many to fear death. One might have acquired an estate of great value. Since he cannot take it with him, he may fear the day when he must leave it.

Atheistic and agnostic tendencies may be responsible for much fear of death. To imagine that, when life leaves the body, we are gone forever, could cause one to want to hang on as long as possible. And, this urge to live will, naturally, cause one to fear death.

You can think of many more reasons why one may fear death. Up to this point I have been attempting to prove to you that fear of death is not a cause, but an effect. There is a reason why one fears death, and if that reason can be learned, it will prove much simpler to overcome it. If you are one of the 95% of people who fear death, give careful thought to what you have read so far. It will help you materially in reaching that mental state where death never occurs to you, at least so far as your individual participation is concerned.

Why Should We Fear Death?

The great majority of peoples on this earth believe in life after death. And, almost without exception, their concept of the hereafter is a place far more beautiful than our present earthly existence. We are taught that our problems cease; aches and pains are unknown, and that living is joyous and free from burdens.

If this is true, and many of our great thinkers accept it as truth, why should we fear that which could easily be accepted as a promotion? This, of course, with exceptions as already enumerated.

I have often tried to analyze my own thinking regarding God and the hereafter. I do not think of God as a being, but I cannot think of life without knowing, to my own satisfaction, at least, that there is a Divine Spirit which controls and regulates this and other universes. I feel convinced that our stay on this earth is not the sum total of our life.

Since to most people life here is a continual struggle, except for intermingled moments of pleasure, it would appear a gross pity to spend a few scores of such years, then have it end.

This book is being written for the purpose of giving you proved, and provable, principles for adding years to your life, and life to your years. It opened with the insistence that you accept the attitude that your life will go on forever. We now come to the second tenet in the regime for adding years to your life:

Accept the thought that there is a hereafter, and that life hereafter will be beautiful.

Should you belong to the minority of people who doubt the existence of a hereafter, there will be nothing wrong in taking sides with the majority and accept the thought that there is a hereafter. You will have everything to gain and nothing to lose by doing so.

Our Allegiance to the Dead

Most people, when a loved one dies, will make a big production of the death. The finest casket one can afford (and often better than he can afford) will encase the remains. A fine funeral home will be selected for the last services; a select burial spot is purchased, or else a fine crypt in a mausoleum; and with well-chosen words on the part of the minister, priest or rabbi, the lifeless body will be sent on its way.

Please do not misunderstand me, I'm not attempting to be satirical. I want to bring the subject of death out in the open so that we can view it without qualms, nor with a superstitious conscience—that makes us feel we are disrespectful to the dead.

The soul of man is man! When the soul leaves the body, nothing remains except the husk. Many keep the gloomy picture of death in mind by constantly visiting the cemetery and weeping over the mound which covers the remains. The casket, and body, in time revert back to earth—which means that nothing of the loved one remains, except the memory.

I avoid attending funerals as much as I can. Not through lack of respect for the departed ones, but because I want to remember them as they were in life—not in death.

I would like to predict what will happen at some time in the future, not very soon, however, because the idea is a bit beyond today's average thinking.

When death occurs, instead of having an orthodox funeral, after the legal requirements have been taken care of—getting the doctor's death certificate, etc., I would like to see the mortician come and, without ceremony, remove the remains and dispose of them in a sanitary manner; the burial spot or ashes not to be of concern to the living loved ones.

Instead of a funeral, wouldn't it be most respectful to have a big dinner—banquet, if you please, at which time relatives and friends would assemble to honor the departed one with eulogy—even anecdotes regarding his life?

Since most of us believe in a life hereafter, wouldn't it be more humane to glorify the life of the departed one instead of his death? Instead of creating an atmosphere of horror, would it be disrespectful to send the soul of the departed one on its way in the spirit that he was graduating to a better life?

Although friends and relatives of the deceased would miss the love, companionship and protection he had afforded while in life, it would be easier on the survivors to feel the departed one had been promoted into a more glorious atmosphere.

Conventional funerals, through necessity, are held within two or three days after death. They come at a time when the survivors are suffering the greatest mental stress; when they are just beginning to understand the truth—that the loved one is gone. The funeral, therefore, inflicts   torture at a time when the bereaved can least stand it. According to my thinking, the "Banquet of Respect" could be held at a time when the remaining loved ones have become sufficiently adjusted to enter into the spirit of the occasion and, instead of being drenched with self-pity, actually rejoice that the departed one has progressed to a well-earned advancement to a higher life.

Physiologically speaking, we have many bodies while on this earth. It is a provable fact that the cells in our bodies are continually wearing out and are being replaced by new cells. With few exceptions, all of the cells are replaced within a period of 11 months. This means that a man of forty has had slightly more than 43 bodies. The cells—making up all of those former bodies—were once animated by our present life principle. We think nothing of their passing from this existence. The hair we cut from our heads; the nails from our fingers and toes; were once alive when a part of our bodies. It would seem absurd to "honor" such physical refuse. Then doesn't it seem that the grief we display for soul-less decaying bodies is a hangover from the ages of superstition?

In this chapter I have been making a feeble attempt to revise your thinking and feeling toward one's departure from this earth. It may be premature to expect you to take the attitude toward the death of others that I have described, but you can change your thinking so far as your own demise is concerned.

You can, through mental discipline, eradicate the fear of death from your consciousness.

You can live as though your life would go on forever.

Love Life, but Do Not Fear Death

In some respects, that which I have been saying in this chapter can seem a bit inconsistent with many of the former chapters. I developed the thought that you can add years to your life, and then devote a chapter selling you on the fact that you should not fear death.

Summary

The opening of this chapter tells you that the fear of death will hasten death. In Chapter Four you are urged to develop a genuine love for life. Now we can take the substance of the former chapter—amalgamate with the thoughts given in this one, and coin a terse axiom: Love Life, but do not Fear Death!

The most important sentence in this chapter is this:

Accept the thought that there is a hereafter, and that life hereafter will be beautiful.

What do you believe happens after death? Whether you believe in heaven, or reincarnation or some other belief system, if you believe that there is a hereafter you will immediately reduce your fear of death.

Note: Several of the following chapters are taken from lectures given in connection with my home study course: Building Mind Power. Of the 22 lectures contained in that course, those which applied to the subject matter of this book were selected.

CHAPTER 9

Developing a Likeable Disposition

Envy's memory is nothing but a row of hooks to hang up grudges on. Some people's sensibility is a mere bundle of aversions; and you hear them display and parade it, not in recounting the things they are attached to, but in telling you how many things and persons "they cannot bear."—JOHN FOS-TER

It has often been said—and truthfully so—that a person is his own worst enemy. This need not be true, of course. It is quite easy for one to be a friend to himself, and if you will follow the simple suggestions given in this Chapter, you will discover to your pleasure that you have found a most worthwhile friend.

In talking about a likeable disposition, I am not assuming your disposition is other than likeable. Everyone, at times, will "blow his top." Some will do it more than others. Every time we do, however, we lose something. It might be respect of others; it might be respect of ourselves.

In writing on this subject, I checked with some of the sages of former years, whose wisdom has been handed down through the ages. I wanted to find what they thought of anger, and particularly of those who displayed it. Their thinking along these lines seemed to follow a common pattern. Confucius, for example, said: "When anger rises, think of the consequences." Seneca expressed it this way: "Anger, if not restrained, is frequently more hurtful to us than the injury that provokes it." Then we read this interesting statement from the pen of Publius Syrus: "An angry man is again angry when he returns to reason." Boyes also referred to reason when he said: "Violence in the voice is often only the death rattle of reason in the throat."

An entire book could be written on the physiological effects of anger; how it actually poisons the system, makes us age prematurely and shortens our lives. These facts, however, are so well known by the enlightened individual, I will take no time in reciting what you already know. You are aware of the damage a bad disposition will do to one's personality.

If, by chance, you may at times display evidences of a bad disposition, most likely, you will be interested in the causes of a bad disposition, and how one may overcome it.

What causes a bad disposition? It is not hereditary. It is not, except in a comparatively few cases, environmental. Let us consider those things which might tend toward affecting one's otherwise pleasant disposition, and knowing the cause, we can change the effect. Here are a few of the contributing factors:—

Guilty Conscience
Unfinished Tasks
Inadequacy
Jealousy and Envy
Laziness
Self-Pity
Poor Health

Guilty Conscience. These words apply to many things— ranging from simple mistakes and indiscretions to robbery and even murder. The latter, of course, does not apply in this case, so we will merely consider the former.

To those who suffer from a guilty conscience, a bad disposition acts as a defense mechanism. They feel subconsciously that, when in the presence of one they have wronged, their display of temper would guard off discussion of anything remotely resembling the reason for the guilty conscience.

Shakespeare said: "Nothing is good or bad, but thinking makes it so." This thought will bear careful scrutiny, and in it a truth may be found which will explain why one could harbor a feeling of guilt.

Many times we accept certain acts as bad, which would be everyday natural occurrences with the average individual.

A woman came to me in great distress. Although she was not an alcoholic, she had reached a point whereby she could not go to sleep at night without having a cocktail. She considered herself as one of the lowest of the low for having acquired such a habit. Her disposition was anything but pleasant, and she was ready at all times to rebuke anyone who might say something not pleasing to her.

A lengthy probing into the life of this unhappy woman revealed many reasons for her present dilemma. In the first place, it was found that her mother was a Puritanical woman who felt that only sinners of the lowest order would touch a lip to anything of an alcoholic nature. Her husband was the type of man who drank nightly before retiring and had convinced his wife she would sleep better it she took a so-called "night-cap."

When she was told that millions of women were doing as she does, without becoming conscience stricken, and also that a cocktail did not induce sleep, but often made one more awake through stimulation, she quickly lost her feeling of guilt and could retire at night without her usual beverage, and drop off into peaceful slumber.

Infidelity can contribute to a feeling of guilt, naturally—but not all offenses are as serious. A man, whose disposition was far from being angelic, was found to maintain a guilt complex—because he had once taken his secretary to lunch. If such an act is ever pardonable, it certainly was in his case. With a jealous wife constantly accusing him of being unfaithful, he reached a point where he felt he might as well have "the game as well as the name." Although he did not go any farther than this one "indiscretion," it was so contrary to his usual conduct, he felt extremely guilty. He became irritable and "snappy" when he was in the presence of his wife, as a defense mechanism, to keep her from bringing up subjects which might have a bearing on his act.

Unfinished Tasks. It would be interesting—and amazing —if we could know how many dispositions "turn sour" because of unfinished tasks.

Many people will start a job and the moment it becomes difficult, or boring, will leave it and turn to something else, perhaps more interesting. We know that these jobs should be completed, so, when we awake in the morning and think of the problems and work ahead of us, these many unfinished tasks come to mind—almost like fingers of scorn pointing to us, and "pop" goes our disposition.

There is a great satisfaction in completing each job we start, before tackling the next one.

I am frequently asked how I accomplish so much, and do so many things. My policy is a simple one and most effective. I start each day doing the difficult, or unpleasant jobs first. There are many reasons why this method proves so efficient. First, I start a difficult job when my mind is refreshed after a good night's rest. Secondly, while I am working on the hard job, my mind is on the pleasant ones to follow; whereas, should I start on the easy ones, I would not enjoy doing them, because my mind would be on the difficult ones awaiting my attention.

Take the right attitude toward everything you do, and you can, by: a. Disciplining yourself to like the job; b. Know you can do it—

perhaps better than it has been done before; c. Unless necessary, do not start another job until you have finished the one you first considered hard.

Inadequacy. I do not know the percentage, but a large portion of our population suffers with that which psychologists refer to as an inadequate type of personality.

Such a person has little or no confidence in his ability to do anything well. When he is working, he dislikes having anyone watch him because, in his mind, he is certain the watcher is inwardly criticizing his work.

After a job is completed, he is not satisfied with it and is sure that everyone will readily discern the inferior workmanship.

It is easy to understand that the inadequate person would be unhappy. He dislikes himself and feels everyone else does.

This chap has an unpleasing disposition because, consciously or subconsciously, he is sure no one likes him, so why should he like others?

Inadequacy is merely an attitude—which, fortunately, can be changed. When one realizes that there is no such thing as perfection and that flaws can be found in every bit of work, regardless of who does it, it is not hard to gain an appreciation of self.

One should never become completely satisfied with the things he is doing, as complete satisfaction retards progress. He should, however, know that his work is at least average—perhaps above average—and that he takes pride in continually striving for improvement.

Jealousy and Envy. Perhaps there are envious and jealous individuals who are happy, although I have failed to find any. The very nature of their affliction is a definite barrier to happiness.

Jealousy usually reflects a lack of confidence in one's self. This is true regardless whether he is jealous of people or things. When jealous of people, he subconsciously feels himself inferior to the one toward whom he focuses his jealousy.

Envy can be linked with inadequacy. We do not envy one for possessions which we know we can obtain.

What has jealousy and envy to do with one's disposition? Plenty! When one is unhappy, he is often manifesting an unpleasant disposition.

Strangely, there are two forms of jealousy. We become jealous of our own possessions—whether physical or material—feeling, others are constantly working toward getting them from us. We are jealous of the possessions of others, feeling they are not entitled to them—and we are.

Laziness. When you saw this word listed among the contributing factors of a bad disposition, you might have felt the word was misplaced. You did not see any connection between laziness and a bad disposition. There is a connection—a most decided one.

A lazy individual usually has a big capacity for wishing. He wishes he could accomplish this or that. He envies the possessions of others and knows he too, could have the same, were he not so lazy.

A lazy person often has a very active mind. He can think of the hundreds of things he could do, but just can't seem to overcome the inertia required to do them.

Laziness is not a cause, it is an effect. If one can locate the cause of the laziness, he can easily change the effect. What are some of the causes?

Badly organized time. One never seems to have the right time for the contemplated job.

Badly organized working implements. Many people will spend more time getting ready to work than the actual job will require. The one who keeps his tools and materials in their proper places can accomplish far more work than the one who spends much time in searching for this and that; and he enjoys his work far more.

Disliking the jobs he is called upon to do. As stated before, this condition can be changed. We are never lazy when we do something we like to do. Learn to like your work and discover how much more you will do—and actually enjoy doing it.

With the lazy person, a bad disposition becomes a defense. Were he pleasant, those around him might have courage to suggest he get his work done. But, if one fears he will have his head snapped off by so suggesting, he is most likely to permit the lazy one to remain just as he is.

Self-Pity. Self-pity is something like halitosis. We seldom realize we have it, and our friends won't tell us. Self-Pity emanates from childhood. When little Mary or Johnny is hurt, attention is lavished on him. He is told how sorry the parents are, and the hurt is usually mended by the gift of a lollipop or a big ice-cream soda. The child enjoys this sympathetic interest. After reaching adulthood, however, he does not have the loving parent to shower him with sympathy, so he does the next best thing—and pities himself.

Very few people understand that grief is a form of self-pity. When we lose a loved one, we grieve, not for the departed one, but for our loss of his love, security, companionship, etc.

Few will agree with this, but on many occasions, illness is acquired—psychosomatically—merely to enlist the sympathy of others.

Self-pitiers frequently carry a chip on their shoulders. They feel they are discriminated against at their jobs and are ever ready to "tell off" those who appear responsible for it.

If they plan an outing and it rains, they take it as a personal affront from the weather department. "This would happen to me," they moan.

Self-pity can be overcome without too much effort it one will determine to overcome it. Consider all obstacles and physical limitations as challenges. Know you are big enough to overcome them and that you'll have a whale of a lot of fun doing it.

Poor Health. Although poor health is not a reason for a bad disposition, it is often an excuse for one. The one below par, physically, will often become extremely unhappy over his plight. He may subconsciously resent those who appear radiantly alive and enjoying life to such an extent that he will have difficulty in being pleasant in their presence.

If your disposition is not good, you are missing much happiness in life.

It is glorious to love life and to like people. If any of the thoughts in this chapter apply to you, discover the reason for your unhappiness and "crankiness" and bend every effort in changing the cause. A new-found happiness will come as a result.

Summary

If you have read this chapter thoughtfully, you have arrived at the conclusion that a bad disposition is related to, and will cause, poor health. And, poor health, you know, is not conducive to long life.

Eliminating a bad disposition will not only assure you a longer life, but will make your life much happier. Add years to your life, and life to your years, so to speak.

You cannot control what other people do, but you can control how you react. Do not blame others for your anger or bad disposition.

Are you smiling? Smiling often will improve your attitude. Try it!

CHAPTER **10**

Mental Concentration

At least one person out of every three coming to me for personal consultation will admit, during an interview, that he lacks the ability to concentrate his thoughts. The words "mental concentration" apply to a characteristic of mind they do not possess, at least according to their own appraisal of themselves.

There are cases where people, through physical limitations or psychological complexes, do lack the ability to concentrate, but these are in the minority. The percentage is so small that you, unless a competent doctor has told you otherwise, can consider that it does not apply to you.

Powers of mental concentration must be developed. It isn't something which we either have or do not have. This is comforting to know because, should you believe you are one who cannot concentrate, you can now accept the truth that you can—and this chapter will prove it to you.

Before showing you how to concentrate, it might be well to understand why you are not able to do so. I am assuming, of course, you are in the group of those who have considered themselves as unable to marshal their thoughts and concentrate on a single subject at a time, or, as Woodrow Wilson said, have a single-track mind. If, by chance, you are one of the fortunate ones who can concentrate, you can pass this chapter by, although the thoughts to be given will help you to understand others and to know why they are as they are.

If you have difficulty in concentrating your thoughts on a single subject, I will be safe in saying that you have frequently used the expression: "I can't concentrate," if not to others, at least to yourself.

Making such a statement is exactly the same as though you instructed your mind to run rampant and flit from thought to thought. Remember this! You will be unable to do anything which you sincerely believe you cannot do. This applies to everything. A poor memory is had by the one who thinks he can't remember. If you think you can't paint, do not try. If you think you can't master a musical instrument, leave it alone. You'll never produce a best seller if you think you can't write. Etc., etc., etc. I'm not implying you will never be able to do these things. But, before you do, your consciousness must change to the point where you know you can, instead of can't.

The subconscious mind has reasoning faculties independent of the conscious mind, but all such reasoning is deductive. Deductive reasoning means reaching conclusions based entirely upon information at hand. As a simple example: One might wish to do a painting job. He has three colors of paint: red, blue and yellow. Reasoning deductively, it would be deemed necessary to limit the color of the finished job to one of these three colors. Inductive reasoning could bring research into use and discover that, through blending certain colors, other shades and hues can be obtained.

It might also be pointed out that in its reasoning, the subconscious mind does not even employ logic. It does not ask questions, such as "how?" Perhaps it would be easier to understand if it were said that the subconscious mind absorbs knowledge by rote; that is, in a mechanical routine way. If you keep repeating the statement, "I can't concentrate," your subconscious mind accepts it as fact, and so long as that thought remains, you simply can't concentrate.

You can record your voice and thoughts on a tape-recorder and the instrument will repeat it back to you— without change. You hear only the words you recorded.

It has often been asked why mind, which is supposed to reflect the perfection of God's handiwork, should accept negative thoughts, and, especially, act upon them. A simple explanation is to refer to the dial telephone. The mechanism in the telephone station—which automatically receives your dialing—and which, without human aid, connects you with another telephone, perhaps miles away, is most intricate indeed. If you dial a number correctly, this mechanism goes into operation and the phone represented by the number you dialed, is called. Should you, through error, dial a wrong number, you are still putting this elaborate equipment into operation, but you become connected with the wrong party.

There are two basic causes for that which we often refer to as being "scatterbrained."

Mentally accepting the thought that you lack the powers of concentration.

Divergence from thoughts through association.

Of first importance is to consider the psychological aspects of mental concentration and the lack of it.

As has been discussed so far in this chapter—if one is to have the powers of concentration, he must become aware of the fact that he can concentrate. This means he must begin seeing himself as possessing the powers of mental concentration.

From this moment onward never think of yourself in any other way except that it is natural for you to concentrate; that, when you direct your thoughts into certain channels, they remain, unmolested by other thoughts, until you have reached a satisfactory conclusion.

There are times when a failure to concentrate is due to dislike for the task in hand. The wandering mind can be an escape. The moment such an individual can find something to like about the job he is doing, he has no further trouble in keeping his mind on it.

Laziness could well be brought up at this point as a reason for failure to concentrate; however, there is no laziness when one is doing something he truly enjoys doing, so, to do what one likes to do . . .or to learn to like what one has to do will automatically eliminate all semblances of laziness.

A feeling of inadequacy at times may be guilty for one's difficulty in concentration. If he doubts his ability to successfully perform a given task, he may have trouble in keeping his thoughts concentrated on it.

I have noticed that those taking up writing as a career often complain of their inability to concentrate. They tell me it takes them an interminable time to write a story, because their minds wander from one thought to another. What a difference there is after they receive a few acceptance-checks. A favorable letter from an editor, accompanied by a check, is like magic. The next story can be written in far less time, and will be much better. You see, confidence in self becomes established, which makes one's creative thoughts flow much more fluently.

Divergence From Thoughts Through Association

A lawyer friend of mine admitted to me that he was worried about himself. He told me he could not keep his mind on the case in hand, it kept going from one subject to another. When he first began the practice of law, he was proud of his mental capacities and that he had perfect mastery over mind.

I no sooner had walked into his office before the reason for his trouble was apparent. His desk was a mass of folders, documents and papers of various kinds. It was hard to see the wood of which the desk was made.

"There's your trouble," I exclaimed, pointing a finger toward the top of his desk.

He looked in the direction I indicated, and, with a puzzled expression asked: "Where's the trouble?"

I suggested to this counselor to remove everything from the top of his desk except the papers pertaining to the case in hand, and I'd wager he could concentrate. You know, without my saying so, that the problem ceased to be a problem.

When this lawyer first started his practice, he had nothing with which to clutter his desk, and, consequently he could concentrate on that which he was doing. As his business grew and he had many files and documents to consider, he permitted his desk to become a depository for all of them. While he was working on one case, his eyes would fall on the papers of other cases, and, naturally, thoughts would enter his mind regarding them. This type of concentration difficulty is called divergence from thoughts through association.

Before beginning work on any creative writing, I like to clear my desk of everything except those things which apply to the subject on which I am writing. Creating such an atmosphere, enables me to write better material in far less time than is normally required.

It is not always possible to free yourself entirely from all interrupting thoughts. The doorbell, the telephone, conversation from others, all are distracting forces. The one, however, possessing self-mastery, who has an awareness that he has great powers of mental concentration, will be able to discipline himself to such an extent that he will direct his attention right back to the original train of thought without too much loss.

A technique which will prove of help in re-establishing thought after an interruption is to review the last thoughts you had prior to the interruption. If you are concentrating on writing and have your attention distracted for a moment, re-read the last several lines you had written. In a majority of cases, your mind will fall right back into the former groove.

A common mistake, made by many, is to create a "disturbance hazard." I mean by this, you become distracted because you expect to be. One may be writing, and have several telephone calls. Disgustedly, he will say something such as: "I'll never be able to keep my mind on this if I am constantly annoyed." Those of us who know anything about the mind and how it operates, will understand that, after a few such expressions, the mind is shot. It will not be able to focus attention on any subject.

If interrupted several times, instead of creating such a hazard, hold the thought that you are happy, because you possess the powers of mental concentration and can—at all times—return your thoughts to the point where you left off at the time of the disturbance.

Exercises for Mental Concentration

An exercise will be suggested which will help materially in developing the powers of mental concentration. These exercises, as it will be easy for you to understand, will strengthen your awareness that you can concentrate.

Place a comfortable chair in a position where you see nothing but a blank wall. Before you, place a small stand or table. On this table lay a book, any book. Your exercise is to relax thoroughly and for a period of five minutes keep your mind on nothing but the book. You do not have to look at it and say: "This is a book. This is a book. This is a book," etc. Think about the book in any respect. You can think about the contents, size, color, name, cover design, etc. It will not make any difference as to how many different phases of the book you think about, so long as you do not let your mind stray from the book. If you know anything about printing processes, you can visualize the book in its making. You can even think about means of selling the book—mail order, through stores etc.

After you have thought about the book for at least five minutes, take a pencil and paper and write an essay on it, based on those things which come to your mind during your period of contemplation. Save this essay.

The next day take a different object for your exercise. Take an apple, orange, or some other fruit. Do the same with this as you did with the book. Think how the fruit grows, the part it plays in nutrition; even the days you gave an apple to the teacher, if you wish. But, keep your mind on the object—or something linked to it.

Write an essay based on this last exercise—and save it. Your essays should contain at least 500 words.

Keep up your exercises daily for a week; each day taking a different object, and each day writing an essay regarding the chosen object. The reason for keeping the essays is for your own satisfaction. After you have completed your last essay, re-read some of the former ones and note your improvement. You will be amazed to discover how you are growing in every respect. You are developing your powers of observation as well as your powers of mental concentration, and, as a bonus, you are even improving in your ability to express yourself well.

There are many phases of mental concentration which are not covered in this chapter, but, after you become concentration conscious, they will occur to you, just as they do to me. For instance, an insecurity complex renders one unable to concentrate as he should, because his mind is constantly on his fear of the future.

Before bringing this chapter to a close, there is one plus in store for all of those who might be on the verge of gaining an age complex. Frequently, when past the so-called middle-age, the lack of mental concentration gives one the feeling he is getting old and out of the running. Having a scatter brain is no indication of age. It merely indicates the individual has not taken steps to organize his thinking.

If you are in the age-bracket above the forties, this chapter will give you such a mastery over your thinking, and, particularly your powers of concentration, you will realize you are turning your calendar pages backward instead of forward. You will realize that, instead of reaching the period where your usefulness will be diminished, you are just beginning your most exciting and productive years.

Summary

The powers of mental concentration are not inherited, they are developed and, unless you make a special effort to develop them, you are not likely to possess that faculty of focusing your thoughts on a given subject without wandering.

One can develop the powers of concentration through practice. Do not feel that "someday" you will practice the exercises given in this chapter—but determine that you will start on them at once.

Become concentration conscious. Instead of wishing that you could concentrate, begin right now in holding the thought: "I am master of my thoughts. I possess great powers of concentration."

Look for ways to reduce distractions. Turn off the television, the phone and other devices.

As a starter in your practice on concentration, close your book—close your eyes—and for several minutes concentrate on concentration, preceding your experiment by repeating the thought before given: "I am master of my thoughts. I possess great powers of concentration."

CHAPTER **11**

Developing a Retentive Memory

A memory is one's life story. It's the sum and substance of every-thing heard or read, and perceived through the other three senses, taste, smell, touch, throughout one's life.

To say there is no such thing as a bad memory would tax the credulity of most people but, so far as the subconscious mind (the real storehouse of memory) is concerned, this is true.

"One of the most striking and important peculiarities of the sub-jective (subconscious) mind, as distinguished from the objective (conscious) mind, consists in its prodigious memory," said Thomas Jay Hudson in his "Law of Psychic Phenomena." He also adds: "It would perhaps be hazardous to say that the memory of the subjective mind is perfect, but there is good ground for believing that such a proposition would be substantially true. Psychologists of all shades of belief have recognized the phenomena, and many have declared their conviction that the minutest details of acquired knowledge are recorded upon the tablets of the mind, and that they only require favorable conditions to reveal their treasures."

The forgetting part of memory lies within the conscious mind, since it has been well established that the subconscious mind retains everything seen, heard or read throughout life. In "Lectures on Metaphysics" by Sir William Hamilton, we read: "The evidence on this point shows that the mind frequently contains whole systems of knowledge, which, though in our normal state, they have faded into absolute oblivion, may, in certain abnormal states...flash out into luminous consciousness. For example, there are cases in which the extinct memory of whole languages was suddenly restored; and, what is even more remarkable, in which the faculty was exhibited of accurately repeating, in known or unknown tongues, passages which were never within the grasp of conscious memory in the normal state."

In the annals of the Psychical Research Society are found summaries of hundreds of experiments which were conducted to prove the claims of the researchers—that the subconscious mind never forgets.

Hypnotists have been able to cause subjects to delve down into their subconscious minds and bring forth detailed descriptions of unimportant events which transpired decades prior to the experiments. I, myself, in my own experiments with hypnotism have found this to be so. I suggested to one subject, a man of 55, while hypnotically asleep, that he was a boy of 15. There was a decided change in his tone of voice, and in his conversation he used the expressions current at the time he was fifteen. He described incidents which transpired during his childhood, which were checked and found to be true, although in his normal state he didn't remember any of them.

In delirium, one will often reveal knowledge he had been exposed to in early life, and, which had not made any impression at all on the conscious mind. A highly interesting case is given by Mr. Coleridge in his "Biographic Literaria." He described a case of a woman of twenty-five who could neither read nor write, and who, during a nervous fever was incessantly talking Latin, Greek and Hebrew, in very pompous tones, and with most distinct enunciation. The case had attracted the particular attention of a young physician, and by his statement many eminent physiologists and psychologists visited the town and cross-examined the case on the spot. Sheets full of her ravings were taken down and were found to consist of sentences, coherent and intelligible each for itself, but with little or no connection with each other.

After much tedious research and inquiry, it was found that in this girl's youth she had become an orphan and was given a home with a pastor. Anxious inquiries were then made concerning the pastor's habits; and the solution of the phenomenon was soon obtained. It appeared that for years it had been the old man's custom to walk up and down a passage of his house into which the kitchen-door opened, and to read to himself, with a loud voice, out of his favorite books. Among the books were found a collection of rabbinical writings, together with several of the Greek and Latin Fathers, and the physician succeeded in identifying so many passages with those taken down at the young woman's bedside that no doubt could remain in any rational mind concerning the true origin of the impressions made on her mind.

Since it has been found true that we have, within our subconscious minds, all of the knowledge we have acquired throughout a lifetime, it would seem logical to conclude that that which we refer to as a bad memory is merely our inability to, at will, bring into consciousness desired facts from our storehouse of memory, the subconscious mind.

The capacity of the subconscious mind, so far as memory is concerned, seems to be limitless. Every wakeful moment of every day, from birth to the end of our earthly existence, we are accumulating experiences, all of which are recorded on the tablet of our mind.

Consciously, our attentions are being directed into endless numbers of channels. There are the multiplicity of sounds on the streets; the ringing of the telephone; conversation directed to us and to others; thoughts flowing in and out of consciousness through association; reactions to physical stimulus, etc., etc.

One will want to recall something from the past, a date, perhaps. The information, due to confusion of conscious thoughts, does not readily come. With the average individual, the usual expression: "I have forgotten," will be said, either audibly to others, or silently to one's self.

To say: "I have forgotten," "I can't remember," "I don't seem to recall," is exactly the same as giving your subconscious mind instructions to withhold the information and not do anything about it.

Each experience one has in failing to bring desired information into consciousness, adds another brick to the mental wall of forgetfulness. It is no wonder, then, that he will gain the feeling that he has a bad memory.

How to Build a Retentive Memory

It is interesting to know that we have, subconsciously, the information accumulated throughout a lifetime, but unless we can bring needed portions of it into our consciousness at will, it does us but little good.

If it were possible for one to have perfect confidence in his memory, he would have no problem of recall at any time. All needed facts would readily be available at all times.

Through constant repetition of such negatives as: "I have forgotten," as before mentioned, a poor-memory consciousness is built up. Before one can improve his memory, steps must be taken to eradicate this poor-memory pattern.

I Have a Good Memory

If you are one of the many who continually comment on having a poor memory, it may sound rather odd for me to suggest that you hold to the thought: "I have a good memory." A moment's reflection, however, will make you realize that your poor memory is the result of seeing yourself as having a poor one. Consequently, your memory will not change, until you reach the point of seeing yourself with a good memory.

At first, you may have difficulty in believing what you are actually saying, but, believe it or not, continue telling yourself time and time again, "I have a good memory." Since it is psychologically true that "motion creates emotion," in time you will know that you have a good memory.

From this moment onward, never, under any circumstances, give voice to the thought: "I have a bad memory." If you wish to recall a bit of information—or an impression, and it does not come into consciousness immediately, instead of closing your memory-door with a negative, keep it open with a positive instruction, such as: "It will come to me presently." You will be amazed to find how infallible your memory really is. In just a moment the information you wish will come into consciousness.

A good memory, therefore, is a consciousness of a good memory; an awareness that you have one.

It has been established that the subconscious mind retains everything one ever reads, sees or hears; and that, to have a good memory, one must develop a good memory-consciousness. There are many things he can do to impress information on his conscious mind—which, in turn, will help materially toward acquiring a good memory-consciousness.

Remember Faces—but Not Names

It is a common expression: "I can remember faces, but for some reason I never remember names." This is not unusual in any respect; in fact, it would be unusual if this were not so. Think about it a moment and you'll agree.

You are introduced to a person. The name is mentioned once—hurriedly—and not too often clearly. You might be with this person for an hour or more, during which time his face is before you. Is there any wonder, then, that by looking at his face for an hour, and hearing his name but once for a second or two, you should remember his face longer than his name?

It is a good practice, when you are introduced to a stranger, to make use of the name as many times as you reasonably can. Instead of merely acknowledging the introduction with: "I'm pleased to meet you," add his name:

"I'm pleased to meet you, Mr. Throckmorton."

It the name is not a common one, it will help to fix it in your mind by commenting upon it. "That is an interesting name, Mr. Throckmorton, is it spelled like it sounds?" Or, you might speculate as to the country from which it descends. Do not feel you will offend when you talk about one's name. To the contrary, it shows you are interested, and it proves complimentary.

When you ask questions, add the name of your new acquaintance, such as: "Do you expect to remain in our city for a while, Mr. Throckmorton?" With such procedure, it is easy to understand that the name Throckmorton will remain with you and that, the next time you meet him, you will not show embarrassment by not having remembered his name.

Remembering Through Association

Association plays a vital part in memory. This means the coming together of two experiences so that the thought of one brings up the thought of the other. On a hill, the brakes of a parked automobile became released, permitting the car to roll down the hill. It crashed into a pole just a few feet from where I was walking. Since then, every time I pass that spot, I recall the accident. It does not come to mind when I see parked cars on other hills.

Most systems for memory-training are based on association. David M. Roth, in his book: "Your Face Is Familiar," uses association of ideas as the basis for his teachings on remembering. For example, if you were given a series of unrelated words to remember, such as: "Hat, Hen, Ham, Hare and Hill," it would take an effort to do so; not, however, by the Roth method. If you were to concoct a story of some kind, tying these words together in sequence, it would take no effort at all to fix them in your mind. For example, you might visualize a large Hat; it rises up and is found to be worn by a Hen, which happens to be carrying a large Ham under her wing. The Hen drops the Ham and a Hare grabs it and runs up a steep Hill. A grotesque illustration you might feel, yet the memory retains unusual pictures longer than usual ones.

We are all familiar with the name, Felix Mendelssohn, the great composer. Can you recall his face? We all know the comic character, Popeye, the sailor man. Can you bring his face to your mind?

Forgetting Because Of Inattention

Although your subconscious mind will absorb all information to which it becomes exposed, unless there is an interest-tie, it will not readily return to consciousness when needed.

Learn to pay close attention to what you are seeing, reading or hearing. And, of equal importance, think while you see, read or listen. Thinking about anything will help to fix it in your mind in such a clear way you can recall it at will.

Our five senses play an important part in memory; sight, hearing, taste, odor and touch. Beauty or ugliness will make an impression on the mind. Sound, either discordant or harmonious will be remembered. A pleasant or unpleasant taste will definitely remain in one's memory, and the same will hold true with odor. Surfaces disagreeable to the touch will be remembered, just as we pleasantly remember the feel of articles soft and smooth.

In your processes of thinking while seeing, reading or hearing, add that which is revealed through your five senses, and you will be giving further ease to your powers of recall.

It's Fun to Have a Good Memory

Have you ever marveled because the desk clerk in the hotel has such an accurate memory? I once registered in a hotel after having been away from it for eight years. The clerk called me by name and while signing the registry card he added: "I believe I can give you the same room you occupied when you were here before." Astounding, you might say, but it is not. The clerk is conscious of a good memory. It is needed in his work and he makes remembering a part of his business.

Frequently hat check girls in hotels and restaurants will put away hats and coats without giving any checks, yet when the owners appear, no difficulty is experienced in immediately locating the correct garment. Not unusual, merely an awareness of a good memory.

The moment you become aware of the fact you have a good memory it will serve you faithfully in any way you wish. Dates, names, facts, all will be ready to pop into consciousness at your bidding.

We Begin Right Now!

Knowing how and why the memory functions, as given in this chapter, will give you an understanding which will still further help you to establish an awareness of a good memory.

At the time this is being written my age is approaching 70, the time when most people feel their memories should fade. My memory is better than it ever has been. I am not bragging in the least. I have a good memory, because I am conscious of the fact that this is true.

You can—and will—have a good memory. In fact, right this minute, it is much better than it was before you began this chapter. It is better because you are organizing your thinking so that you will remember.

Summary

Having a good memory is another way of saying you have an awareness of a good memory.

You have within your subconscious mind everything you have read or heard throughout your lifetime.

Stop thinking and saying, "I have a bad memory." By continually holding to the thought: "I have a good memory," you will develop one. You will be surprised and pleased to find facts coming into consciousness when, as and if you need them.

Practice focus and attention. Make an effort to remember things you want to remember, such as names.

Repetition can fix information in your memory. When you want to learn something, go over the information several times, allowing for breaks in between each session. When possible, get the information in more than one form. For example, reading text, listening to audio, etc.

This one chapter will prove to be priceless if you take it seriously and follow the suggestions given.

CHAPTER 12

Peaceful Sleep

Sleep sweet within this quiet room,
Oh thou who e'er thou art,
And let no mournful yesterday
Disturb your quiet heart...
Forget thyself and all the world,
put out each feverish light.
The stars are watching overhead.
Sleep sweet! Good night! Good night!
—ELLEN HUNTINGTON GATES

Sleeplessness usually results from bad bedtime habits.

Tossing and turning for long periods of time after retiring is more frequently psychological than physiological. If, however, you have difficulty in sleeping at night, you should first consult your doctor to learn whether it is your mind, or some bodily ailment which is keeping you awake.

If it is the former, this lecture will prove of great value to you. If it is the latter, be guided by your doctor. So, the thoughts and suggestions given to you under the title of "Peaceful Sleep," are based upon the assumption that you are in normally good health.

I will spend no time in talking about sleep, and what it is from a physiological standpoint. In fact, you are not interested in knowing what sleep is; what you want to know is: How to go to sleep and rest peacefully.

A fault discovered is half overcome, it has been said, to which I heartily agree. So, let's begin by considering a few of the reasons for sleeplessness.

Worry. This is probably the Number 1 enemy of sleep. We worry about finances; about health of ourselves and family; about our jobs or businesses. We worry about wars and rumors of wars. We translate sounds into thoughts of burglars. We worry about the impressions we did or did not make on those with whom we have had recent contact. If you will reflect over the worries which have kept you awake in the past, you will be able to list far more types of worry than I have.

Solution. Be logical! Realize that worry cannot, in any way, help the condition over which you are worrying. A sleepless night—with a mind of worry—will rob you of the stamina which could help you to combat the causes of your worry.

"Most worry is a lie," wrote a great philosopher. "Seldom do the things you worry about materialize." he added.

Think back over the things you have worried about in the past, and you will agree with this wise man.

If you'll apply the principles you have learned so far in this book, you will find that the things we worry about are not causes of worry at all. They are challenges; opportunities for us to grow as we find solutions to our problems.

Tonight, and every night hereafter, instead of worrying go to sleep with the thought: "While asleep, my subconscious mind will find a solution to my problem, and tomorrow will guide me to do the things which will eliminate the condition which might otherwise cause worry."

Worry, you know, means one is holding mental pictures of things he does not want, instead of things he does want. So, as you go to sleep, visualize the ideal condition you are seeking instead of the one existing, and know that, until you do go to sleep, you are not giving your subconscious mind an opportunity to work on your problem.

Living With Your Work. Many men and women will carry their work to bed with them. For hours they will re-live the day just ended thinking of the things they did do, but should not have done, and thinking of the things they did not do, but should have done. After spending sleepless hours with the past, they will change to the future, thinking of things they will do, and things they will avoid doing.

Solution. Before retiring at night, take a few moments and review the day's work. If there was anything not pleasing to you, decide what you will do about it the following day or in the future. Make use of that subconscious mind of yours—which never sleeps—and permit it to work for you while you sleep. Know that a good night's peaceful rest will let you awaken in the morning, refreshed and ready to start a day of great accomplishment.

Jealousy. It is pitiful how many hours of sleep the green-eyed monster has taken from men and women. Such hours of sleeplessness are miserable too. We toss and roll as we imagine our happiness—and security—being taken by another.

Solution. Jealousy usually indicates one of two things: selfishness or inferiority. As you retire at night, realize that refreshing, restful sleep will give you the charm which makes you unafraid of competition. Remember! The more you trust others, the more that trust will be deserved.

Envy. Not all of us, but a goodly number of people, upon hearing of the good fortune of a friend or relative, will stay awake for long periods of time, wondering why they never get the breaks. They envy others who have better jobs, better homes, better automobiles, etc.

Solution. Envy is negative. To envy one for a possession he may have indicates that you doubt your own ability to obtain that which you are envying. Instead of envying, use the power you already possess toward acquiring the object of your envy.

Guilty Conscience. A guilty conscience does not always indicate that the one so affected has committed a crime or a breach of conduct. Our conscience might bother us if we feel we have been negligent toward those near and dear to us. Or, our conscience might disturb us if we feel we have been neglecting ourselves—so far as the improvement of the body is concerned.

Solution. A guilty conscience is caused by something which happened in the past. It is beyond the power of anyone to re-live a day of the past. Let bygones be bygones and determine that you will forgive yourself for your mistakes of the past—and profit by them—so that you will not make similar mistakes in the future. Go to bed with a song in your heart, because of your resolve regarding the future.

Laziness. The lazy individual loses sleep in two ways. He will think about the opportunities he has missed, and is missing due to laziness. He will also spend time in thinking of ways and means whereby he can avoid doing other things he should be doing.

It has often been thought that a lazy person sleeps more than he should, because he is lazy. He can ordinarily drop into sleep at times when he should be occupied, but will stay awake when he should be sleeping, because of the dislike for his apathy toward work.

Solution. You have learned by now that there is no such thing as physical laziness. All laziness is mental. When we dread doing a certain type of work it is because we are not interested in it. It bores us. Learn to like that which you have to do. Decide it will be done a bit better than ever before. Again, as I said a moment ago, we cannot relive the past. If laziness has been one of your drawbacks, retire with a promise to yourself that, in the future, you will find something to like about everything you are supposed to do and that you will take delight in doing it well.

Hatred. In conducting studies on sleep and the causes of sleeplessness, it has been noted that one with a heart of hatred never sleeps as well as the one whose mind is at peace with himself and the world at large. This person has difficulty in going to sleep—and when he does, he is tense and rests but little.

Solution. Hatred is a poison which works on both your mind and your body. If one could realize the damage which can be done by hating, he would understand that he cannot afford to hate. Remember! Hatred never harms the one hated. The hater is the only one who pays the penalty. And, does hatred keep one awake? On one occasion a man did something toward me which "burned me up." I went to bed and for two or three hours kept myself awake by just dwelling on the action which brought about the hatred. After carrying on this inward "hymn of hate" for a good portion of the night, I realized I was harming no one but myself. I even asked myself the question:

"Wouldn't that fellow be glad if he knew how he was keeping me awake?" In other words, I was really allowing him to bestow more injury upon me. Realizing the futility of lying awake—just hating—I actually whispered a prayer asking that he be blessed and guided to do right by his fellow man. This act dissolved my hatred, I dropped off into restful sleep and woke up in the morning actually sympathizing with the man instead of hating him.

Planning Ahead. So far, this is the only constructive reason given for sleeplessness. Progressive, far-sighted people will usually spend many of the hours in which they should be sleeping in making plans for the future. As admirable as this trait appears, we are developing a weakened physical condition which will later hold us back from doing the things we might plan to do.

Solution. In planning for the future, why not take full advantage of the great source of intelligence and power contained within your subconscious mind? Retire with a thought such as: "While asleep, my subconscious mind will draw from my experiences of the past, and from them formulate practical and progressive moves for the future. I am happy in anticipation of my continual growth and achievement!" You can, if you wish, be more specific as to your future. If you have a definite objective, include it in the bed-time instruction to your subconscious mind. For instance: "While asleep, my subconscious mind will evolve the proper steps I should take in obtaining wider distribution for my product (mention name), and I will be guided accordingly."

Creating. The inventive type mind, whether the inventiveness may run along the lines of patentable ideas, designs, story material, subjects for painting, etc., will frequently use the bed as a place for the germination of the ideas.

Solution. What was said for "Planning" may also be said for "Creating." When you stay awake and attempt to create, you are using but a small portion of your mind. When you permit yourself to drop off into peaceful, relaxed sleep, after having given proper instruction to your faithful servant, the subconscious mind, you are utilizing your greatest mental powers. I do my best writing early in the morning. As I retire, I tell my subconscious mind: "I will sleep peacefully tonight, and as I do so, my subconscious mind will develop a good theme for my newspaper article, and in the morning, as I write, thoughts will flow to me enabling me to write a good article in a short period of time. Many times, in the morning, as I place a sheet of paper in my typewriter, I will not know what my theme will be.

By the time I have the paper set, ideas begin to come into consciousness—and continue to do so, until the material is completed.

Fear of Death. Last, but by no means least, is the fear most people have of dying. If one's health is not good, he fears death through physiological means. He might fear death through an accident, such as a plane, train or automobile; or even as a pedestrian. And, at night, when everything is dark, and we have a feeling of aloneness, is the time when we give vent to such fears.

Solution. Love life, but do not fear death. I know of no one who has more right to want to live than I have. My home life is happy; my future is bright and getting brighter; my health is good; yet, with all of this, I give no thought whatsoever as to the day when I will leave this plane of existence.

As you learned in Chapter Eight, fear of death hastens death. When we have a pain or an ache, instead of looking for the cause, and trying to correct it, we worry about it—and associate it with possible death—and we become frantic. Live as if you had an assured life-span of at least 125 years. Then, no matter what your present age might be, you are young in comparison with the time you have set for yourself.

Eliminate the fear of death and you will have eliminated one of the common causes for sleeplessness.

Problems, fears and worries are greatly magnified at night. With eyes closed—and in a dark room—your entire attention is focused on that which is keeping you awake.

In the daytime, with your eyes wide open, the object of your sleeplessness, when viewed in comparison with all about you, loses much of its importance.

Many people actually prepare for a sleepless night before they retire.

"Oh, how I dread going to bed. I just know I'll not sleep," they moan.

You know that to hold such thoughts is exactly the same as instructing your subconscious mind to keep you awake; and it obeys. Look forward to retiring. Think how good it will feel to be disrobed and be able to stretch out and relax in a comfortable bed. Know that soon you'll be fast asleep, gaining strength and energy.

Coffee is often blamed for loss of sleep, and in many cases, wrongly so. It has been said that the stimulating effects of coffee are worn off in about two hours after it is taken. If you have dinner at six, the coffee-effect should be gone by eight. Yet, with most people, if they do not retire until ten or later, they do not sleep, "because they knew the coffee would keep them awake." This sleeplessness is psychological and not due to the beverage.

There are a few things you can do that will be conductive to healthful sleep:

Do not have your bed located where lights from the outside will fall upon the face.

Do not have your bed in a draft, but do see to it that your bedroom is well ventilated.

If there are any unavoidable sounds or noises which might keep you awake, get the right attitude toward the sounds—instead of resenting them—and they will no longer bother you.

Some people find it necessary to live in neighborhoods where there is considerable street noise. Resenting it will keep you awake. Acting indifferent toward the many sounds will cause you to forget them.

"I just can't sleep with all that racket," one might proclaim. Of course knowing the mind and how it operates as you and I do, we understand that such a statement is literally instructing the subconscious mind to keep you awake!

As a young man, I slept in a tent in a mining camp close to a mill which operated on a 24-hour basis. The roar from the grinding machinery was terrific. But, I became so used to it, should the mill close down during the night for any reason, the silence would awaken me.

Summary

Reducing the text of this chapter to a capsule formula for sleep, I might say:

Know it is no effort for you to drop off into peaceful sleep. Do not dread going to bed, because you fear you will not sleep. Look forward to retiring, because of your healthful rest and peaceful sleep.

Form good bedtime habits:

Go to bed at the same time every night, and get up at the same time each morning.

Eat dinner at least three hours before bedtime.

Do not watch television or use computers or other devices with screens before bedtime.

When you are in bed, you should be sleeping. Do not use your bed for anything other than sleep or sex.

Knowledge is of no value unless you make use of it. This is definitely true regarding what you have learned about sleep. This very evening put the suggestions to use and tomorrow you will be enthusiastically telling your family what a wonderful night's rest you had, and how well you feel.

CHAPTER 13

Increased Energy Through Relaxation

When I was just a child I had a puzzle which consisted of a series of wood strips, each bearing several notches. These strips, when put together correctly, would make a solid mass about the size of an orange. The puzzle was to take it apart. The strips were so interlaced, and interlocked, it appeared that one must break it to disassemble the pieces. But, there was one strip which proved to be the key.

Remove that one and the rest would fall apart.

The analogy between this puzzle and relaxation is this:

Tenseness, the antithesis of relaxation, is responsible for many ailments. Tenseness of the leg muscles can be responsible for cramps. Tenseness of the intestinal tract can interfere with the peristaltic movement of the bowels and can cause constipation.

Close and tense your hand, then quickly open it. Notice how you had interfered with the flow of blood. If tenseness can hamper the flow of blood, it naturally can affect the heart, which is responsible for the flow of blood.

In the realm of color, there are three primary ones, red, blue and yellow. Any two of them blended together will produce a new color,

124 • SWEETLAND & STUCKER

referred to as secondary color. It two secondary colors are blended, you get another one, called a tertiary color.

Many physical ailments result from a combining of two or more simpler ones. Borrowing the nomenclature of color, we might say that two primary ailments could cause a secondary ailment, and two secondary ailments could create a tertiary ailment.

Now I can make use of the puzzle illustration. Just like the puzzle has a key block which unlocks all the rest, we can think of tenseness as a key ailment. Remove it by relaxing, and many secondary and tertiary ailments will disappear.

Tenseness an Ally of Age

In a study made of those who are showing age prematurely, it has been found that in nearly every case the individuals so afflicted were tense most of the time. In fact, if you talk to them about tenseness, they will reply with some remark, such as: "How I wish I could relax!"

Those who retire in a tense condition do not sleep well, and when they do sleep, do not rest. They awake in the morning feeling almost as tired as when they went to bed. Is it any wonder, then, that such people show their age years before they should?

Eating when tense is an insult to the human body, because food does not properly digest under such conditions. Indigestion causes many other complaints, constipation, headaches, etc. And, do these conditions add years to one's life and life to ones years? There is only one answer.

It would be impossible for me to overemphasize the importance of relaxation, particularly as it applies to age. One might accept every suggestion given so far in this book and yet fail to add much to his life if he remains tense most of the time.

A man in his early fifties came to me bemoaning the fact that he was always tired. He was tired when he awakened in the mornings.

He had difficulty in doing a day's work because every effort he made required more energy than he had. At night he would retire and go to sleep through sheer exhaustion.

It did not require more than ten minutes with this man to determine the cause of his trouble. He was constantly tense.

As he would sit in a chair, he'd invariably grip the arms as though they were trying to get away. His neck muscles were as taut as violin strings. Movements of his legs were jerky.

I explained to my visitor that when one is tense he is burning energy; when relaxed he is storing energy.

"But I can't relax," he almost shouted. "My muscles are so tight they will not loosen up," he added.

Most tenseness starts with the mind as you will learn later in this chapter. I knew that the difficulty this man was having was more mental than physical. I wanted to discover the cause of his trouble.

With his consent, I experimented with hypnosis. He was a difficult subject to hypnotize, because his mind was as tense as his body. After a lapse of half an hour devoted to relaxation and sleep suggestions, he succumbed to light sleep.

Through a progress of regression, taking him back, mentally, to his childhood years, the cause of his mental tenseness was uncovered. It seems that, as a boy, this unhappy man was afflicted with what psychologists call acrophobia, a fear of high places. His parents, in trying to make him overcome this tendency, actually enhanced it by forcing him to ascend to heights and look far below. On a visit to New York, he was taken to the tower floor of a skyscraper. The family also took him on a vacation to the Grand Canyon of Colorado where he was led to the edge of the canyon to gaze thousands of feet below.

Our bodies reflect our minds. Here was a case where a man had his mind so imbued with horror pictures, his body could not relax.

Before awakening him from his hypnotic sleep, I told him, over and over again, that he enjoyed high vantage points, where the world below him presented a glorious vision. I next created a subconscious awareness of relaxation; that he had perfect control of his body and could relax at will. I concluded the hypnotic experiment by suggesting that he would retire early that evening, relax thoroughly, and enjoy a restful night's sleep.

The next day he phoned to me stating he had slept perfectly and had not felt as well in many years.

To make sure the benefits of my experiment would be lasting, I repeated it on four other occasions.

The results were little short of amazing. When this man first came to me, although in his early fifties, he looked like a man well into his sixties. The last time I saw him he didn't look fifty, but several years younger. Now then, let me ask; will this man add years to his life and life to his years?

Tenseness Is Psychosomatic

Before giving you the reason for this suggestion, let me ask you to try an experiment. The moment you finish reading this paragraph, lay your book aside and close your eyes. Imagine yourself on the roof of a very tall building and you are standing close to the edge where you can look down to the street below. The automobiles look like tiny toys. People on the sidewalks appear as moving dots. As you stand there, fascinated by the view, you lose your balance and fall.

Did you notice yourself tensing as you imagined you were hurtling through the space?

Here is the reason for this experiment. I want to prove to you that your body responds to your mind; that, unless your mind is relaxed, your body will not relax.

Books and books have been written on relaxation. Most of those I have read treat tenseness as being purely physical. They give all sorts of exercises for relaxing the body, and for a while they do relax the body. Do you know why? Because during the exercises your mind is on relaxation. But, after your mind reverts to the many things which have caused the tenseness, you will find it returning.

This brings us to the potent fact that, unless you can relax your mind, you will not be successful in relaxing your body.

Fear is, perhaps, the most prevalent cause for mental tenseness, particularly ingrained fears which have assumed the proportions of phobias. Fear of losing one's job with the awareness of consequences will cause one to tense mentally each time he thinks of it. Fear of the death of a loved one, one whom you are dependent will likewise affect one's mental equilibrium.

Fear of illness, accidents and disease—all will contribute toward a mind of tenseness. Fear of loss through fire, storms, earthquakes, wars, etc., will not be conducive to mental tranquility.

Worry, as covered so thoroughly in Chapter Seven of my book I Can, is definitely responsible for mental tenseness. Since worry is defined as "holding mental pictures of things you do not want," it is easy to understand how such negative mental pictures could prevent one from comfortable relaxation.

It is now obvious that learning how to relax requires consideration of many factors. The formula for relaxation, therefore, can be expressed as follows:

Fear. Eliminating fear, as such, and disciplining the mind so that, instead of fearing, it will acquire understanding.

Worry. Learn to dwell, mentally, on the things and conditions you want, not those you do not want.

Through physical education, train every fiber of your being to respond to your mental pattern.

Acquiring the Art of Relaxation

Have I made it appear that to learn to relax will be a major task, requiring much study and great application? I didn't intend to. I first wanted to give you an idea why most people have difficulty in relaxing. The rules I will give you are simple indeed, if you follow them step by step. All mathematical problems, as complex as they might appear to be, are based upon the simple rules of addition, subtraction, multiplication and division which you learned in the elementary grades at school. Mastery over tenseness will come through application of very simple rules.

Gain an awareness that you can relax. Instead of wishing that you can relax, know that you can. Hold to the thought: I CAN relax. Repeat it to yourself many, many times daily. If you find yourself getting tense, instead of thinking: "I wish I could relax," dwell on the thought: "I CAN relax!"

Of course, knowing that you can relax is not enough. Knowing that we CAN do a certain thing does not imply that we are doing it. All of us CAN do many things which we are not doing. So we must go beyond the knowledge that we can relax, and bring into being the fact: I AM relaxed! This secondary stage of awareness must come after mastery of fear and worry. So long as the mind is ruled by fear and worry, the use of the words: "I AM Relaxed," would be farcical. So, let us give due thought to our enemies—fear and worry.

Fear. If one would learn to be rational regarding the objects of his fears, he would be able to quickly dissipate his fears.

I was visited by a man whose fears were showing. The expression on his face displayed a disturbed mind. He wanted help. He wanted me to give him a bit of peace of mind.

"Let us take a few of your fears and analyze them," I suggested. After a moment's reflection, he told me about a man he dreaded meeting. He owed him a sum of money and had not been able to keep his promise in paying it. Every time the telephone rang, he would wince, fearing it was his creditor calling. He shuddered when the mail arrived, thinking there might be a threatening letter from the man he owed.

"What would happen," I asked, "if you were to face this man and tell him frankly why you have not been able to make a payment, and just what you intended to do about it?"

"Well, I don't know," he drawled, after thinking it over a moment or two.

"Then why don't you try?" I urged.

He did. To his amazement, he found his creditor not only pleasant, but cooperative. Here was a needless fear. Naturally, the elimination of this and other fears, enabled this man to relax mentally, and likewise physically.

A mother lived in mortal fear that her small children would play in the streets and get run over by an automobile. Whenever they were out of her sight, she was extremely nervous and tense. "Use every reasonable precaution you can," I advised, "then trust in God that they will be kept from harm."

"It was not easy to do," boasted this fine mother, "but from what you said I could see that my fears did not help a thing, but did harm me, and even caused me to be irritable toward my husband and children due to my tense state." She conquered her fear and, of course, gained much happiness and peace of mind.

You might not concur with my next idea in this regard, but I am inclined to accept the thought expressed in Job 3.25: "For the thing which I greatly feared has come upon me." This verse is, no doubt, responsible for the proverb: "Fear attracts that which is feared."

Have you ever used the expression: "I was afraid of that?" You probably have; it is a common expression, especially after something has gone wrong. Is it just a coincidence when you fear something, and it happens?

Those who know anything about the mind and how it operates know that fear and worry actually set the laws of nature in motion to bring about that which is feared.

So that it will not appear to be bordering on some Hocus-pokusism, permit me to explain why fear attracts that which is feared.

First let me make one thing very clear. Nature does not punish one by causing bad things to happen. You, yourself, attract them to you. If you should hold the negative mental picture-patterns in mind, nature doesn't ask you if you are sure this is what you want.

You automatically put the forces to work in making a reality of the condition pictured. As already mentioned in Chapter Ten, if, in dialing a number on your telephone, you happen to make a mistake and dial the wrong number, the head of the telephone company does not give you a wrong person just to punish you. No, you dialed a wrong number, and in doing so, put the complicated mechanism at the telephone station into operation and the telephone corresponding to the wrong number was called. If you hold a negative mental picture, you merely put the forces of nature to work in reproducing that picture in your being and affairs. In other words, you mentally dialed a wrong picture and you got a wrong result.

I could devote many pages in explaining why our minds work as they do in this regard. I could refer you to the countless successful experiments in extra sensory perception conducted by Dr. J. B. Rhine of Duke University. You would understand how our thoughts attract the object of our thinking to us—whether negative or positive. I could go into quite some detail as to how fear of accidents will make one "accident prone" and he actually attracts accidents. But, for the sake of brevity, I ask you to accept and be guided by that which I believe to be a fact: Fear attracts that which is feared.

Through physical education, train every fiber of your being to respond to your mental pattern.

Early in this book you learned that man is a mind with a body. In considering relaxation, it is important that you know this fact.

Right now, raise your right hand. Wiggle your fingers! Open and close your hand two or three times. Now then, did you have any difficulty in doing this? No! You did it because you knew that you could do it. You gave a mental instruction to your fingers and hand to do certain things and your fingers and hand obeyed. All muscles of your body will respond in a like manner. If you instruct the muscles of your arms or legs to relax and you know they will obey, just as you were able to wiggle your fingers, you will find that the muscles will relax.

Better Sleep Through Relaxation

"I sleep soundly all night, yet I am always tired when I awake in the morning." Have you ever heard this expression? One can sleep without being relaxed. And, when you are tense all night, you are not restoring energy, with the result you are almost as tired in the morning as when you retired.

I can give you some simple rules which will enable you to sleep quickly, sleep peacefully—and awaken in the morning refreshed.

Do not use will-power in trying to go to sleep. The more you will yourself to sleep—the wider awake you will become. After you have retired, just realize how good it feels to be in a comfortable bed with your clothing removed; and don't care if you sleep or not. Yes, that is what I mean. Do not care about your sleep. You are comfortable and resting.

Remove all the cares of the day from your mind. There is nothing you can do about them while you are in bed, so forget them for the period of sleep.

Go through a relaxation routine, starting with your toes and covering every part of your body, actually instructing your muscles and joints to relax. It is more than likely, you will be asleep before you finish.

After a night of peaceful, relaxed sleep, you will find yourself arising in the morning with an abundance of energy. And, if you start the day well, it is quite likely to end well.

Keep Youthful Through Relaxation

In learning to relax, do not forget the facial muscles. Most of the unpleasant expressions you find on faces, were put there through tenseness. The vertical lines between the eyes are put there when you wrinkle your forehead while thinking or working. The so-called crow's feet at the corners of the eyes are put there by squinting. Hard lines are carved around the mouth through anger and, of course, a bad disposition.

A smiling face is a relaxed face. You have heard much about the value of a smile so far as personality is concerned. Now you know that smiling will also enhance your beauty. So, do not forget to have a pleasant smile on your face, in connection with your relaxation regime.

Summary

Tenseness is an ally of old age. Tenseness is one of the major causes of many bodily ailments, and will do more to hasten age than almost any other thing.

Tenseness is more mental than physical; it starts in the mind. Continued mental tenseness will bring about physical conditions which definitely affect one's health and cause him to age prematurely.

Become relaxation conscious. Think in terms of: I CAN Relax, and you'll soon reach the state where you can proudly boast: I AM Relaxed.

Both meditation and hypnosis can help you learn how to relax. Try them. You may find that you prefer one over the other, or you may find that each has its place in your life. An easy way to get started is with one of the recorded guided meditations or hypnosis sessions.

If you are as happy as I think you'll be after reading this chapter, you will want to turn right back and re-read it before continuing with Chapter Fourteen.

CHAPTER 14

Overcoming Fatigue

Note: This chapter deals with psychosomatic fatigue. If your energy is continually at low ebb, first, before following these suggestions, have a careful examination by your doctor, and be guided by him or her.

Most people get tired because they expect to get tired. If they awaken in the morning, facing a day of many duties, they will start the physical processes developing fatigue, because they anticipate by the end of the day they will be exhausted. And, they are usually right. By night-fall they are tired. In such cases, it has been the mind—more than the work—that made them tired.

When we take vacations, my wife and I enjoy transcontinental motor trips much more than spending our time inactively in some resort.

On one occasion we laid out a most comprehensive trip. The route circled the United States: starting out from San Francisco, heading south, then through Arizona, New Mexico, Texas, etc., into Florida; up the eastern coast through New York and New England, then across the Northern part of the country to the Pacific Northwest, then south to our home. The route covered about 9,000 miles. Thirty days were allowed for the journey, and since I had accepted many speaking engagements, we had to run on a carefully planned schedule.

Before our departure, friends and acquaintances by the score were predicting one of two things; either we could not maintain such a schedule, or, if we did, we would arrive home completely exhausted.

We completed the journey according to plan. "Aren't you just about dead?" was the question put to us constantly by those who had come to see if we were still able to sit up and talk about the trip.

Were we tired? Not a bit! We reached home mid-afternoon and felt so good, we unpacked the car and put everything in its place before retiring that night.

This story is not intended as bragging. We did nothing others cannot do. But, we started the trip with mental pictures of enjoyment, not fatigue. And we did enjoy every mile, and at no time did we stop to rest due to fatigue.

With cross-country driving, where traffic is light, there is little reason for getting tired. Very little energy is required to drive the modern automobiles. The seat in the car is as comfortable as the sofa at home. When one learns to relax at the wheel, driving can be pleasant and actually healthful, because the constantly changing panorama of on-coming scenery stimulates one mentally.

On one of our transcontinental trips, we left New York at the same time a friend was departing for the same destination. We all had dinner together the evening before the take-off. This friend was dreading the journey—because he knew it would be so tiring—averaging nearly 400 miles per day. We planned on averaging 500 miles per day.

In San Francisco, after all of us had completed our journey, we again got together to compare notes.

Our friend's prediction of fatigue had materialized. "Boy was I exhausted!" he declared as he started to talk about his trip. He told us how he would drag himself to bed each evening. Arriving at his destination, he was so worn out he could not have stood up to another day's driving. He was really peeved at us when we told him we reached home "as fresh as a daisy."

In this case, both of us reproduced the conditions we visualized before our departure. Our friend pictured fatigue and he achieved it. We looked forward to an enjoyable, restful trip, and we had one.

Two Types of Fatigue

Natural Fatigue.
Psychosomatic Fatigue.

Natural Fatigue is weariness resulting from bodily or mental exertion, according to the Oxford Universal Dictionary. It is easy to accept fatigue as being weariness from bodily exertion, but there is no such thing as mental fatigue according to Bruce Bliven, who said:

"Laymen often speak of 'mental fatigue' or 'brain fog' thinking—that long, concentrated mental effort produces tiredness in the brain itself. Your brain is not like your muscles. Its operations are not muscular but electrochemical in character, comparable in part to a direct current wet-cell battery.

"When your brain appears tired after hours of mental work, the fatigue is almost certainly located in other parts of your body, your eyes, or muscles of your neck and back. The brain itself can go almost indefinitely."

I am inclined to agree with Bliven.

Nature requires rest and relaxation for the purpose of restoring worn tissue, and to accumulate energy for coming activities, but it is amazing how much less time we will require for rest, once we learn how to relax during all periods when relaxation is possible.

Many people, by being tense throughout the entire day, will end the day utterly exhausted. Their dinners do not digest properly, because fatigue retards digestion. Dinner over, they are too tired to enjoy any recreation. Physical weariness is not conducive to restful sleep. From physical exhaustion, poor digestion and loss of sleep, it is easy to understand how many other ailments would come into being as a result.

An ideal condition is to reach bedtime with that which I refer to as "wholesome fatigue." (It is when you look forward to crawling under the covers of a comfortable bed, to relax for a peaceful night's sleep.)

Psychosomatic Fatigue is that condition first talked of, where the mind generates fatigue, because we expect to get tired.

There are several things one might do to avoid psychosomatic fatigue:

Learn to like the things you have to do.

Start the day doing the most difficult things first.

Keep your mind on the ease with which you work.

Relax at each opportunity.

Fill your mind with happy thoughts.

Learn to Like the Things You Have to Do

A woman once took issue with this statement. "I can't learn to like scrubbing and washing," she blurted defiantly.

"You can, so long as you have to do it," I explained.

I told her the story a woman once told me as to how she learned to like that which she had to do.

"I went to a movie," she said, "and the picture was a marine one. In one scene a number of "gobs" were down on their knees "swabbing the deck," and as they did so were singing, in rhythm with their work."

"They appeared so happy," she continued, "I decided to do as they did when I had to scrub floors. It was like magic! As I scrubbed, I would sing just like the sailor boys did. I did the job in half the time normally required, and it did not tire me a bit."

You can find something to like about everything you do. Discover new ways of doing it. See if you do it a bit better than it has ever been done before. Think of ways to do the job a little faster than it has been done before. You may discover ways of doing the work more economically than before. You see, as you begin to view a piece of work as an opportunity to express yourself, it loses its aspect of drudgery.

Start the Day Doing the Most Difficult Things First

This has been touched upon in previous chapters but for different purposes. Now we make the same suggestion, as it bears upon fatigue.

There is a great satisfaction in seeing jobs, which have appeared as difficult, being completed. Before tackling a tough assignment, one will often spend much time thinking about it before actually starting. As the minutes, and sometimes hours, roll by, the magnitude of the job grows in the mind of the one expected to do it. It reaches the proportions of a monumental task, and psychosomatic fatigue begins to develop.

Lay out your days so that the hard, or unpleasant jobs will be started first. As you start the day, instead of holding "dread thoughts," and wasting much time in hesitating getting started, jump right into the work holding such thoughts as: "This job will be easy and pleasant and I will enjoy doing it." The first thing you know, you will be well into the work, and surprising enough, it will have proved to be easy and pleasant.

Keep Your Mind on the Ease With Which You Work

Each time you say to yourself: "This job is hard," you are making it more so. Your subconscious mind—accepting the thought—will cause the work to consume more energy than otherwise.

If you have been making the mistake of building a "Hard job consciousness," for a change, try holding to such thoughts as: "I have abundant energy to do this job well, quickly and without fatigue." It will surprise you the difference it will make. You will complete the job in less time than you would normally take, and you'll end it with energy to spare.

Relax at Each Opportunity

As you learned in Chapter Thirteen, when relaxed, you are storing energy; when tense, you are burning energy.

Evening fatigue is caused by being constantly tense throughout the day. You exhaust your store of energy. If, on the other hand, you relax every opportunity you get, even it for only a few minutes at a time, you will have drained off far less energy than normally, with the result you reach home at the close of the day, ready to enjoy your dinner and an evening of pleasant recreation.

Fill Your Mind With Happy Thoughts

Many stores, factories and offices have music during working hours. It has been found that the music has a tendency to bring harmony in one's mind and lighten one's burdens. Time passes more pleasantly, and with less fatigue to the worker.

Psychological studies among workers have shown that one with a gloomy mind will acquire more fatigue and do less work than one with a happy mind.

Worry and fear usually dissolve happiness. You can discipline yourself to hold to happy thoughts that will deny entrance to worry.

If you have a problem disturbing you, permit your subconscious mind to work on it while you work on other things. You can give your subconscious mind instructions, as you have already learned, by holding to such thoughts as: "While I am occupied on this job, my subconscious mind will conceive ways and means of solving...(mentioning the specific problem). After doing this, take your mind off the problem and feel happy in the knowledge that an intelligence greater than that of your conscious mind is working on—and will solve—your problem.

Guard Your Health

That subconscious mind of yours will direct every organ of your body to function in a way assuring you good health, if you but direct it to do so. But, remember, in order to properly carry out those instructions—your body must have the essential vitamins and minerals. Select your food with care and, if you have any doubt at all regarding your intake of vitamins and minerals, add the food supplements which will give them to you.

Think in terms of health. See yourself radiantly healthy. This, together with the right food intake, will make your entire being vibrate with health.

Fatigue and Age

When one is tired, his mind is ordinarily on the negative side. If he should be well along in years, he is likely to translate his fatigue in terms of age. And when we think we are getting old, we are instructing our subconscious minds to bring about that very condition.

Sometimes our age causes us to think in terms of fatigue. We allow ourselves to get tired because we feel we should tire easily at our age. Then the fatigue adds still more to the consciousness of age. And on and on it goes—the vicious cycle—age inducing a consciousness of age!

A man of my acquaintance—age 62—knew that he was in the midst of old age, because he tired so easily. After a long talk with him, I found he expected that a man of his age should get tired easily. After telling him most of the things I am telling you, he changed his thinking completely with amazing results.

"I'm younger today than I was ten years ago," he later told me, "and strangely, I do far more work than I did before talking to you, and I don't get tired a bit," he added with enthusiasm.

Boredom will often cause fatigue. When one becomes bored with what he is doing, he will get tired, (psychosomatically) because that will give him an excuse to stop what he is doing.

Psychological studies have shown that, after five hours devoted to any one task, one will become bored with it. If one can change what he is doing before the end of a five-hour period—his vitality will keep up far longer than otherwise. Remember that!

The subject matter of this chapter is of vital importance. Once you learn that most fatigue is psychosomatic, you will add much to your satisfaction of living, and you will be adding years to your life and life to your years.

Summary

In most cases, one gets tired because he expects to get tired.

If you start your day with the feeling you have a very heavy program ahead of you and, particularly if there are duties you do not like to perform, you are most likely to end your day dog-tired.

Get plenty of sleep, and start each day excited about what lies ahead.

If you can start the day with a happy attitude, glad you are capable of performing the tasks ahead of you, the day will end finding you in high spirits and feeling fit.

When there is something you dread doing, do it first. Get it out of the way and you will be free to do the things you enjoy.

Come up with ways to make the things you have to do more fun. Get a friend to join you. Sing while you work. Make a game out of it.

In connection with fatigue, keep in mind the valuable points you learned in the previous chapter on relaxation.

CHAPTER 15

Happiness

Happiness lies in the consciousness we have of it, and by no means in the way the future keeps its promises. —*GEORGE SAND*

Correctly speaking, to say you are happy means you are lucky. The word "happy" is taken from the word "hap" which means luck. Although I do not believe in luck as the name implies, I do believe the happy one is lucky.

In this work, my reference to happiness refers to a state of well-being, resulting in enjoyable or pleasurable satisfaction. We might think of it as blessedness, suggesting deep or refined enjoyment arising from the purest affections. One may even soar to a state of felicity, denoting intense happiness, which has more formal or elevated connotations.

As much as one might yearn for happiness, it is gratifying to know that it is within the reach of all of us, because happiness comes from within. It is not an external condition. Our happiness is not contingent upon people or things, but rather our attitude toward people and things. For example: One person might be profoundly happy under a certain set of circumstances. Another one might have reason for gloom under identical conditions. As a simple illustration: Mrs. A. and Mrs. B. may receive gifts of the same kind. Mrs. A.'s gift appeals to her and she is happy. Mrs. B.'s gift, an exact duplicate of the other gift, does not appeal to Mrs. B. and she is unhappy. You see, it was not the nature of the gift which induced happiness or gloom, it was the attitude the recipients had toward the gifts.

At one time, I maintained an office on a floor high up in one of the familiar New York skyscrapers. From my window I could plainly see the activity on many of the busy streets.

In New York, there are two uniform dates when people move. Offices are usually leased from May 1st to May 1st. Residences are leased from October 1st to October 1st.

On one occasion, it was October 1st, I peered from my window, and in every direction one could observe moving vans parked in front of apartment houses. People were moving in; people were moving out. Some were moving from the city into the suburban areas; others were moving in from the country to the city.

"Why are these people moving?" I asked myself. Although there undoubtedly were numerous reasons, one answer would be prevalent, I am certain; "to find happiness."

Weary, unhappy city people feel that the hustle and bustle of the Metropolis is responsible for their morose state of mind. Weary, unhappy suburban people feel that the lack of activity is responsible for their boredom.

You cannot rent happiness! You cannot obtain it by changing locations. Unless one takes happiness with him, he will not find it at any destination he might have planned to reach.

In the Adirondack Mountains in north-eastern New York exists a hunting and fishing club. The club is an active one during the spring and summer months, but in the winter this place is entirely deserted, except for the caretaker.

"How do you stand living here alone throughout the long winter months?" a guest asked this custodian.

"I wouldn't change places with the richest man on Broadway," he reflected philosophically. "Lonely? Why man, I do not know the meaning of the word! The deer coming down to the lake's edge stop by my cabin for a sweet cookie I have ready for them. The jackrabbits and cotton tails visit me to make certain I have saved morsels of greens for them. The birds love me because they know I love them. Yes, sir! My life is one of contentment and joy."

Ask the first hundred people you meet how they would like to live entirely alone in a mountain cabin throughout the winter. How many would admit liking such an experience? Probably no one.

The man I referred to finds happiness in a type of life which would prove disagreeable to most people.

Many will claim they cannot be happy doing the things they have to do, and, of course, in a majority of cases, these people are wrong. Should such people change their work, they would soon again be unhappy.

Happiness is not in doing the things you like to do, but in liking the things you have to do.

"How can I be happy when...?" many will ask, and then enumerate dozens of reasons why they feel they cannot, under the circumstances, be happy.

"Because you do not want to be happy!" I replied to one such question. I was looked at as though I had not taken the plight seriously. Then I proceeded to disprove her arguments by pointing out case after case of men and women in circumstances much less abundant than hers, who were ideally happy.

At one time, while broadcasting from Detroit, I received an urgent call from a shut-in. This young lady was confined to her bed 24 hours of every day. Her body was paralyzed to such an extent she could not raise her arms high enough to touch her hair. She was blind. If anyone ever had a legitimate excuse for self-pity, it certainly belonged to this young lady. But, was she unhappy? Just the opposite. Why did she want me? A man whom she knew had just been defeated in a political race. This man had plenty of money and did not need the office, but the little shut-in was so sure he was unhappy, she wanted me to do what I could to make him happy. This little lady instead of feeling sorry for herself, kept happy by thinking of ways and means of making others happy.

Maurice Maeterlinck said: "An act of goodness is of itself an act of happiness. No reward coming after the event can compare with the sweet reward that went with it." This is as much as to say: Happiness comes from giving happiness. As frequently as I have used this expression, I must admit that it is true only under proper conditions. Happiness comes from giving happiness—when we give it unselfishly and with no thought of reward other than the warm glow which comes to the heart when we have been able to sense the joy our act has imparted.

Do you know there are certain types of people who do not want to be happy, and yet who will bemoan the fact that they are not happy? A strange paradox, isn't it?

The foregoing statement seems to call for an emphatic "Why?"

There are many answers to this question, but permit me to digress just a moment before giving the reasons. What I am attempting to do in the first part of this chapter is to examine happiness and learn as much as we can about it, so that, when we might not be feeling jubilant, we can look for the cause—and change the effect.

In enumerating some of the reasons for unhappiness, you will recognize a few of those listed in one of the previous chapters which dealt with one's disposition, and the reason for an unpleasant one. Let us consider the factors contributing to unhappiness.

Guilty Conscience

Self-Pity

Envy

Selfishness

Timidity

Worry

No Religion

There are many, many more reasons for a lack of happiness, some of which will occur to you as you read this chapter. Those listed, however, will suffice to show you that, once we learn the reason for unhappiness, it will not be difficult to change the cause, bringing about the desired effect: happiness!

Guilty Conscience. When one suffers from a guilty conscience, he consciously or subconsciously feels he is not entitled to be happy. Should he catch himself smiling, he will suddenly stop, feeling happiness is not for him. As you learned earlier in this book there are two things one should do when he finds himself held back by a guilty conscience:

Correct the condition which is causing the guilty conscience, if at all possible.

If there is nothing you can do to make amends for any mistake you have made, then forgive yourself. Cleanse your heart and soul of any ill-will you have been holding against yourself. Declare to yourself that you will profit by your mistakes and prove to be a better citizen and friend as a result of them.

I have made lots of mistakes in my life; many which cause me to blush as I think of them. But, instead of holding myself back by constantly dwelling on my mistakes, I, through my books, magazine articles, syndicated columns, radio and television programs, have attempted to guide others so they will not make the same mistakes. Through this attitude I can safely say that, in a small way, the world is a better place in which to live, due to my mistakes.

The right appraisal of the cause of a guilty conscience will enable you to dissolve it, and actually gain happiness.

And, as you learned in Chapter 5, freeing yourself from guilt will add years to your life and life to your years.

Self-Pity. The self-pitier is one to really be pitied. As you have learned, self-pity is a hangover from childhood.

We can't be happy and pity ourselves at the same time.

And strange as it may seem, the one who indulges in self-pity really does not want to be happy. When one pities himself, he does so to enlist sympathy from those with whom he comes in contact. To appear happy would discourage sympathy. Should this type of person catch himself smiling, he will suddenly change because, after all, we do not sympathize with those who are happy, do we?

Envy. Envy is a destroyer of happiness. If one finds another person living a bit better than he is; with a better home, finer automobile, more clothing, a larger income, etc., he is likely to become sullen—because he does not possess such luxury.

The mere possession of wealth and luxuries is no assurance of happiness. Some of the most unhappy people I know are rich—so far as worldly goods are concerned. On the other hand I know many who are destitute in comparison and who are extremely happy.

I am not belittling wealth. I believe everyone is entitled to the luxuries of life as well as the necessities. I am, however, insisting that without the right attitude toward worldly possessions, we will fail to find happiness.

"Anticipation is greater than realization," it has been said, and quite truthfully so. This may, at first, seem a bit discouraging if I should imply that once you acquire something it will mean less to you than when you were thinking about getting it.

There is an explanation to this apparently odd mental quirk. Achievement brings one of the greatest satisfactions in life. When we desire something badly enough to turn on our mental power and physical strength to make it a reality, our most profound happiness comes as we see our guided efforts bring our objectives into realization. Naturally we will enjoy that which we created; whether it be a simple project, or a giant business. But the master-thrill came as we saw our ideas taking on tangible form. And, one should not consider the attainment of an objective as a destination. It is just a plateau where we pause for happy contemplation of what we have accomplished, and to build mental and physical stamina for the next objective—which has been peeping over the horizon as the former one neared completion.

Selfishness. Did you ever hear the story of the snake which put its tail in its mouth, and ate himself up? As grotesque as this picture is, it bears resemblance to the selfish person.

Selfishness, just as the name implies, means pertaining to self. When one tries to attract everything to himself; although he does not consume himself, as was the case in the ludicrous story, he does destroy his happiness. A selfish person is trying to live in direct violation of the fundamental laws of nature. All nature is on the giving side. The trees, the flowers, the birds, the sunsets, all are on the giving end. There is an inexhaustible supply of everything.

The more we give the more we get. If one is not getting enough in this life he is not giving enough, because all receiving is preceded by giving. Have you ever seen a selfish person who was happy? I haven't.

Timidity. There is a close relationship between timidity and selfishness. Timidity is largely due to self-consciousness or, reversing it, consciousness of self. When we can reach that point where we think of ourselves as contributing toward the happiness of society, instead of merely seeking happiness for ourselves, we will be well on the road toward freedom from timidity.

Develop a "you" attitude. Think of people in terms of "What can I do to make you happy?" instead of "What can you do for me to make me happy?"

"The greatest thing in the world to me is me," said a renowned philosopher. Herein lays the solution to the overcoming of timidity. If, when with another, you would realize that the greatest thing in the world to that person is himself, and then act accordingly, you will have no difficulty in overcoming timidity. You will find yourself thinking in terms of making him happy instead of remaining so self-conscious you are afraid to be with others.

Worry. Worry has already been described in foregoing chapters as being the mental pictures we hold of things we do not want, instead of pictures of the things and conditions we do want. Worry and happiness cannot live under the same mental roof. While it is true that worry will destroy happiness, it is also true that, if one will give expression to a sufficient amount of happiness, it will crowd out worry.

We might think of worry as the clouds and happiness as the sunshine. In my many plane trips I have frequently flown over the clouds. Above, the sun would be shining brightly. The ground would be dark and dreary due to the clouds. Yet, to those on earth, they know that, if the clouds were to go there would be sunshine. One should likewise understand that, if the clouds of worry should be dispersed, the sunshine of happiness would come through.

A woman once came to me with a long face, drenched with worry. Life was almost unbearable—according to her. I asked her to approximate the number of hours she had spent on the cause of her worry. She came up with a rather large figure. I then suggested to her to try an experiment. She should, for the time being, lay her worry aside and spend her time in finding a solution to the worry. She'd keep a record of the number of hours she would spend on this constructive side of the picture. Do you know what happened? She later came to me with a perfect solution to her problem—and the time taken was only a fraction of the amount of time she had formerly spent in worry. This is something for all of you to keep in mind, whenever worry is around to rob you of your happiness.

Religion. Everyone should have a religion, and live according to it. One without religion is like a lost soul wandering alone in the wilderness.

With a religion you have a Presence constantly guiding you and giving you the strength and courage to remain erect at all times, even in the face of obstacles.

Study the face of the one who sincerely believes in his religion. There is an unmistakable gleam of happiness which soars to the realm of ecstasy. Such a person has no problems. He faces every condition as a challenge, and knows that—with his God—all things are possible.

The belief that youth is the happiest time of life is a fallacy. The happiest person is the person who thinks the most interesting thoughts, and we grow happier as we grow older. —WILLIAM LYON PHELPS

Summary

Happiness is a state of mind. You can be just as happy as you decide to be.

Happiness is not in doing the things you like to do, but in liking the things you have to do.

The only way you can have happiness is to be happy.

This being true, realize how much you are losing in life without giving expression to the happiness you already have.

You will not only gain much in life—spiritually—but will be more successful, since it is true that a happy mind is more constructive than one permeated with gloom.

Start right this moment in giving your smiling muscles a bit of exercise.

CHAPTER 16

How Well Is Well?

Perhaps you have never asked yourself this question. It will prove interesting to think about it a moment, and you may start a train of thought which will carry you to a state of happiness you have not known before. When do you think of yourself as being well? When you are free from pains and aches? When you can do your normal work without exhaustion? The questions which could be asked are numerous, but the "64 dollar question" could be, even if you are free from pains and aches, and are able to do your regular work without exhaustion, would it be possible to feel still better?

The pinnacle of well-being is when you feel vibrant, mentally and physically, and you can throw your entire enthusiastic self into anything you might do, whether it be work or play; when your mind is free from worry, because you accept the problems of the day as a challenge instead of approaching them with fear; when your heart is free from hatred, because you have eyes which look only for the good in others, and when your todays are better than your yesterdays—and your tomorrows are looked toward to with joyous anticipation.

Following are ten simple steps for radiant Mental and Physical Health, which will give you a new concept of how it feels to be really well.

Step 1. Have an Incentive to Want to Be Actively Alive—on Top of the World

We can do almost anything if we really want to. This applies to physical well-being as well as to anything else. We might go through the motions of doing things intended for better health, but, unless our actions are backed by a burning desire to success, we need not look for spectacular and glowing results.

It's wonderful to feel good, to have that up-and-at-'em feeling, but, before we will take steps to get this way, we must have a mighty good reason for doing so.

So, Step Number 1 is to get the incentive; the reason for wanting to have every fiber in you being effervescing with vibrant energy.

I'll offer a few suggestions, merely as thought-starters, but for the real answer, explore that mind of yours to find just what you would like to have or be; an objective, the attainment of which would bring into your life a satisfaction heretofore dreamed of, but which you never expected to be yours.

Would you like to be a power in your community? Would you like to have the type of personality which sways people? Forcefulness is not a question as to how you pitch your voice, or how loud you talk. It is a reflection of a mind alert and a body dynamically alive and vigorous.

Would you like to have a large circle of admiring friends? Would you like to be the one singled out for your opinion and advice, because there is something about you which seems to spell authority?

Would you like to be elected to important posts in your lodge or club, because of your personal magnetism?

Would you like to climb higher in your job because of your dependability?

Perhaps your desires might run along the lines of personal accomplishment. You may have said: "I would take up the study of music, if I felt better." Or, it might have been painting or the mastering of one of the many crafts.

I may be a thousand miles from anything which even nearly approaches that which could be your incentive. You may be single and would give anything for the right mate, but feel you do not have the youth or physical attractiveness to prove of interest to the opposite sex.

But, regardless what your desires are, get an incentive to WANT to be on top—physically and mentally, then you will be in a position to get the maximum good from the steps to follow.

Step 2. Know You Can Gain Better Health and Live Longer!

The only people who have ever accomplished anything are those who knew they could. To approach any task with doubt in your mind as to your ability to do it is a certain step toward failure.

Buoyant health is not something we acquire by luck. It is a reflection of the way we think and the way we live. Bodies which creak with aches and pains are not given to us by Fate as a punishment of some kind. We have them because of the way we live and think.

A mistake which is made by most people is to the effect that the price we pay for a joyous state of well-being is so high, the reward is not worth the effort. How utterly wrong!

One might say that sacrifice is part of the price we pay for a vigorously alive body. But is it? Let us take a few of the habits as an example. To those who smoke to excess and whose hands shake like palsy if they are without a smoke for a few moments; would it be a sacrifice if they were to practice moderation to the extent that a smoke would be enjoyable, instead a means to keep from suffering? To those who drink to excess; is the intense suffering from a hangover the reward one gains from the habit? Would it be a sacrifice to suggest moderation; that a drink would be taken now and then for sociability, instead of shearing one of all semblances of culture and refinement?

At first thought it may be hard to believe that we make more sacrifices with an ailing body than we do to have and maintain a glad-to-be-alive body. Think it over and you'll quickly agree. Reflect over the many things you could and would have done, had you felt like it. Think of the places you would have visited—had you the physical stamina and mental spirit to do so. And, think of the countless hours of feeling just "half fit."

Your judgment tells you that, if you embark on a program aimed toward glorious health, you can accomplish it, so, this step is to KNOW you CAN gain better health and live longer.

It may be necessary to resort to a bit of mental discipline in developing a better health consciousness. If, for years, you have been seeing yourself as one under par physically, it will take an effort to get yourself to a point where you know, beyond doubt, you CAN enjoy radiant health. Motion creates emotion, we learn, so, for a few days hold to the thought: I CAN gain robust health.

Of course, accepting the thought that you can gain better health is not enough. You must take the steps which will make better health a reality. In other words, the realization that good health is within your grasp, must be backed by action. The following simple steps will produce astonishing results.

Step 3. Get Your Mind in Order!

Today the word "Psychosomatic" is frequently heard in connection with illness. Doctors are including many, many ailments in a long list of those which are originated in mind. This casts no reflection upon the mind so far as sanity is concerned; instead, most psychosomatic conditions result from fear and worry.

Stomach ulcers are talked of most as originating in mind; "strain" we call it, but what is mental strain other than worry over certain conditions, or our vivid fear that we will prove to be inadequate to cope with them.

My definition is that worry is an evidence of doubt in our ability to solve the problem which is causing the worry. Perhaps if we look at it from this angle, we might stiffen our spines a bit and prove to ourselves and others that we are bigger than the object of the worry—and will do what is necessary to change it.

Realize that worry never helps anything. To the contrary, it impairs health and blocks happiness.

Self-Mastery is a reward which comes to the one who can conquer fear and worry—and they are easy to conquer if one will accept and act upon the truth: "Worry Prevents Our Doing the Very Thing Which Would Provide the Means to Prevent the Worry."

Step 4. Learn the Things You Should and Should Not Do!

A sage once said: "Success comes from doing the things you know you ought to do, and not doing the things you know you ought not to do."

It could wisely be said that invigorating health would result from following this same advice. But, of first importance is to know exactly what you should and should not do. Where can this consequential information be obtained?

The moment we become imbued with any thought, we almost become a magnet for information on that subject. We are attracted to books and periodicals covering various phases of it. Our minds and thoughts dwell upon it.

"A fault discovered, is half overcome," I learned when just a boy. I believe if I were to take exuberant health as an objective, the first thing I would want to know is the condition of my body at present. I would, therefore, let my doctor give me a head-to-toe examination, so I could learn many of the things I should and should not do regarding my physical being.

An architect visualizes his ideas as they come to him. At his drawing board, and with his instruments, he develops his thoughts objectively. Since we are architects of our own beings and affairs, it would be well to begin by listing those things we should and should not do in our pursuit of glowing health.

A plan of action should be conceived which would include activity on the things we should do, and discipline in avoiding the things we should not do.

Naturally our program of action will include supervision over the food we eat. But here and now let me say that robust health does not mean giving up the things you like in favor of those you do not enjoy.

Vitamins and minerals are as essential to vibrant health as light and water are to plants. To have a deficiency of either vitamins or minerals means living in a body under par physically—and one which will break down many years prior to its destined time.

A startlingly large percentage of people are suffering from malnutrition, not that they are eating too little, but the foods they do eat are deficient in the elements necessary for health.

Selecting a diet of items recognized for certain vitamins and minerals is no assurance that they are being obtained. Good virgin soils hold an abundance of the minerals essential to good health, but, in all parts of the country these minerals are being used up much faster than nature, or the farmer can put back again. They are used up by over-cropping, carried away by erosion, washed out by rains.

Vitamins are not food. They do not turn into blood, flesh and bones, or supply energy with their own substance as foodstuffs do. They act instead as important links in the chemical processes by which the body turns food into tissues, removes waste products, and produces energy. Without vitamins these vital processes could not go on.

Selecting food with care is always a wise precaution, but the one determined to have scintillating, glad-to-be-alive health, will not risk getting all essential elements from foodstuffs presumed to contain them, but will make certain of a balanced diet by adding food supplements obtained from a reliable source.

Step 5. Develop an Enthusiasm to Do and Not to Do

Acquiring the facts given in Step 4 is essential in reaching our major objective: Radiant Mental and Physical Health, but, merely acquiring this information is not enough. We must develop an enthusiasm for carrying through; for putting into operation the plans which will assure radiant health.

There is one word, common to most of us, which has been responsible for many of our failures in life. That word is: "tomorrow." How often do we learn of something which would be of help to us, and we resolve to do it "tomorrow?" And, of course, "tomorrow never comes."

If you have been reading with a serious mind, you are enthusiastic—right now! You are beginning to see vistas of thrilling happiness with a sparkling mind backed by a dynamic body. Problems which heretofore have been worries to you, now appear as a challenge. But, as you peep behind the curtain and envision your new future, do not allow the element of procrastination to usher forth the thought of tomorrow as a starting point. Start right now, the moment you lay this book aside. The start need not be a physical one, doing something the eyes can see. The start can be your resolve; your resolution that, since your rightful heritage is vibrant mental and physical health, you, from this moment onward, will do everything within your power to make it a part of your existence. The reason for this is obvious.

Step 6. Take Years Off Your Life Through Your Actions.

Motion creates emotion. The man or woman who makes pals of their children and who enters into the activities of youth, will remain young far longer than the parents who live according to the traditionally old-fashioned mother and father.

We can't act young without feeling young, and when we feel young, we are putting the processes of Nature to work toward making us young.

Dancing, swimming, rowing, hiking are a few of the activities which promote physical well-being. But, right here, in connection with these pastimes, there is a thought of considerable importance. Do not do anything merely because you think it will be good for you to do so. Since, as we learned in Step 2, there is a definite relationship between mind and body, learn to like the things you do. If you dance, enjoy it to the fullest extent. Then you will gain the combination of psychological and physiological benefits. This holds true with all other forms of exercise. The more you like them, the greater will be your benefit.

Our clothing plays an important part in the way we feel. If we wear garments that are drab in color, we do not feel as cheerful as when we inject an element of color in our apparel. Although it is always imperative that we dress in good taste, one should not select garments which will suppress emotions.

What did you enjoy doing ten, twenty or perhaps even thirty years ago? Try to renew your interest in it. You may find the years rolling off your age as you do so.

Step 7. Go on a Mental Diet!

Again referring to psychosomatic ailments, those physical conditions which emanate from mind, I would dare to say that a mental diet is more important than a physical one.

Negative thoughts produce negative reactions. An old philosopher once said: "Seek thy comrades among the industrious, because the idle will sap thy energy from thee." As to whether or not this is true, recall to mind visits you have had with those whose conversation is confined to subjects of gloom and disaster. Remember how you left feeling quite gloomy yourself. On the other hand, think of time spent with the optimistic, hopeful person, and you will remember leaving very much inspired, and feeling like doing things yourself.

Discipline yourself to think in terms of health and happiness. Select reading matter which will inspire you to climb to greater heights.

Do not indulge in negative conversation. When you write letters, see how much encouragement you can give, instead of making them dissertations of woe.

The secret of happiness is not in doing the things you like to do, but in liking the things you have to do. I am repeating this truth, because of its tremendous importance, and I want you to accept this thought as a forward step in your mental diet.

In Step 5 you determined to abandon the word "tomorrow" from your vocabulary so far as procrastination is concerned. This will apply, definitely, to your mental diet. You are on it—right now!

Step 8. Teach Others How to Have Radiant Mental and Physical Health.

It is true that happiness comes from giving happiness, and that to teach others how to gain radiant mental and physical health would make us extremely happy; but there is another reason for the suggestion given in this step.

We can't successfully teach anything to others without setting an example. It would be incongruous to tell others how to be joyously alive and exuberant, while we, ourselves, were to drag along as if only half alive. Certainly not! We would want to show what life is meaning to us, so that it would be an inspiration for them to follow our example.

Since charity begins at home, enlist the support of the various members of your family to join with you in attaining radiant mental and physical health.

Start a movement among those with whom you work, not only for the good you will be doing for them, but for what it will do for you.

Practically everything we do in life is based upon habit. We live according to the habit patterns we have created. Some habits are good—some are otherwise. In following this step, you are subconsciously training yourself to create and live according to new and highly beneficial habit patterns.

Step 9. Live Correctly!

These two words could lead one into many different avenues of thought. Live correctly could refer to your food, to your habits, to your mode of living.

"Let your conscience be your guide," is the meaning I wish to convey. To talk about our relationships with others might seem a far cry from the rudiments of good health, but psychologists know that the things we do that challenge our self-respect are reflected in our physical condition.

A person who is not dependable never enjoys the vibrant health common to the one who is respected for his dependability. An unpunctual person is not on top of the world physically. Why? Because something psychological from within is disturbing. Subconsciously he loses a certain amount of self-respect, and a psychosomatic illness is usually the result.

In connection with the subject of this step, I cannot neglect disposition. One with a bad disposition never enjoys vigorous health. I have explained in previous chapters how bad dispositions undermine happiness and even success, but from a health standpoint, ask your doctor. Ask your doctor to explain how anger actually releases a poison in the blood stream which retards the digestion and encourages any of a long list of maladies.

Anger and reason do not go together—as evidenced by the fact, that when we're angry, we say and do many things we later regret. You can see, therefore, that by giving in to anger you are retarding your progress, and doing immeasurable harm to your physical being.

Step 10. Be Happy.

A prominent and successful doctor once said that a happy person is seldom ill, and when so, responds to treatment much faster than other people. You will have no difficulty in agreeing with this doctor if you will reflect a moment. You know you feel much better, physically, when you are happy, than you do when you are sad and depressed. You also know that when you are not quite up to par, and something happens to cause great elation, you at once feel better. This will show you why the two words: "Be Happy" make a fitting conclusion to these ten steps for Radiant Mental and Physical Health.

Happiness comes from within. You now have—and always will have—all the happiness there is. To be happy is merely to express happiness. And to express happiness is to take a great step forward toward acquiring inexhaustible, glowing health.

when we are satisfied with the thoughts we are thinking and the things we are doing!

There is a distinction between satisfaction and peace of mind. You are warned against becoming contented with your status of life, because contentment with what one has done with his life thwarts progress.

Discontent has often been classed as the mother of invention. One with a constructive mind will, if discontented with anything, give serious thought to find ways and means of improving it.

Can one have peace of mind and be discontented at the same time? Decidedly yes! However, there are many factors involved. To be discontented without doing anything about it, would give anything but peace of mind. A few of the contributing factors responsible for peace of mind with discontent are:

- Urge to eliminate the cause of the discontent.
- Confidence that you can contrive that which will bring about the desired improvement.
- Action on your part in overcoming the cause for discontentment.
- Satisfaction of achievement.

One can possess peace of mind without accomplishing anything. There is a type of an individual who, given sufficient security regarding the future, even though that security be no more than a modest assured income, can have peace of mind. Such an existence, however, is not to be desired.

A thought provoking quotation from the works of Seneca is: "Nothing is more dishonorable than an old man, heavy with years, who has no further evidence of having lived long except his age." We read in Genesis that Methuselah lived to 969 years, but that is all we know about him.

Reading this book is evidence of your desire for self-improvement; an urge to build a life which would justify its right to existence and occupy an important niche in the variegated pattern of humanity.

Knowledge is of no value unless you make use of it. A woman who was making a transcontinental motor trip said she had seen so much wonderful scenery she was becoming satiated and could no longer enjoy what she was seeing. It was not until after she had returned home to relive her various experiences that she could fully appreciate all that she had seen. This could be more or less true with this book, so many exciting facts regarding the fullness of life have been given, one could easily become bewildered in the glow of the new life unfolding and might overlook some of the elements responsible for the transformation. This book should have added immeasurably to your storehouse of knowledge. This knowledge becomes of value to you as you make use of it, as it becomes a part of you.

The moment you complete this book, review every chapter. Do so with a sense of rejoicing. As you come to each subject, approach it with elation, that it represents a possession of yours, one of the contributing factors to your peace of mind.

I am not guessing when I say you have far more peace of mind now than you had before starting on Chapter One. However, I will be much happier to know that you have complete peace of mind.

To assure yourself of this supreme blessing, I have laid out a series of checkpoints to enable you to make certain you have, and are, doing everything essential to your complete peace of mind. Many times, when driving a nail through a board, the part which protrudes on the reverse side will be bent over to "clinch" the nail so that it will not come loose. These checkpoints might be considered as "clinchers" to assure you that you will have and retain Peace of Mind.

Live In The Present. Look at your past as having been a training period for your new and exciting future. If you have made mistakes in the past, (and who hasn't?) instead of letting them haunt you think of them as object lessons.

Some people have enjoyed a larger measure of success in their earlier life than they are experiencing at present, and they become discouraged as a result of it. Should this apply to you, feel grateful that you were at one time capable of achieving success and that at this present time you possess all the knowledge you had then, plus added experience; all of which will enable you to climb to even greater heights in the future.

Love Life. Start each day—from the moment you awaken—with joy in your heart for the new day which is dawning, and keep your heart filled to overflowing with a zest for life and all it represents.

Be grateful for those conditions normally looked at as problems, because to you they are no longer problems. They are opportunities for growth and expansion.

Love every phase of nature: the trees, the birds and the flowers.

I once was a guest in a most palatial home. There were several million dollars' worth of rare paintings. In examining them I was impressed with the fact that every painting represented something which you or I can see in the original at all times, and without cost. There were paintings of landscapes, seascapes, buildings, and people. Every place you go, you will see beauties and wonders, if your vision is attuned to receive them.

Be Forgiving. Forgive those who have wronged you. Forgive yourself for mistakes you have made. Peace of mind and a heart of hatred can never live together in the same body.

Retire at night with gratitude in your heart, because you do not dislike anyone. If someone continues to wrong you, sympathize with him, because you know he is not happy. Since hatred injures no one except the one hating, do not permit the folly of another to harm you.

It is not easy to accept the thought expressed in St. Luke 6.29 . . . "And unto him that smiteth thee on the one cheek offer also the other." It pays, however, and handsomely.

At one time in my life, I lost a sizeable contract because a young man had lied about me. Later this same man needed a reference from me in order to secure a very important job. He was sure he would not get the job because it seemed certain that I'd "get even" by giving him a bad reference. To his surprise, I helped him to get the position. Did I lose? Certainly not! This man felt so humiliated—and so grateful—that later he helped me to get a contract even larger than the one he formerly caused me to lose. Suppose I had not "turned the other cheek" how would I have gained? This man would still be an enemy, hurting me every chance he'd get; whereas due to my attitude I made a friend of him and gained materially by doing so.

Face The Future Without Apprehension. It was once said that our mistakes of the past and fear of the future are why the present is so difficult.

Fear of the future is usually due to one's lack of confidence in himself to cope with situations as they arise. When you motor in a country not familiar to you, every time you come to a turn in the road there is a happy expectancy as to the type of scenery about to unfold before you.

Life is an adventure, if we assume the correct attitude toward it. We can look forward to each new day with confident expectation.

Be Calm. A nervous jittery feeling of haste is not characteristic of a mind of peace. "Haste makes waste!" is more than an axiom—it is a fact. When we rush any work, we become careless, we make mistakes—and end up with our nervous system tied in knots.

I once sat at a lunch counter, right opposite the short order cook. He was preparing food for at least thirty people at all times. I was amazed with his efficiency and calmness. He did not seem to be working fast, yet he was keeping all the patrons satisfied. The secret of this man's dexterity was his manner of making every movement count, there were no lost motions.

An efficient person is one who has a place for everything and everything in its place. This means there is no lost time in trying to locate the things you need.

A man who organizes his time and who is master of self will have no difficulty in maintaining calmness, thereby lessening fatigue and maintaining peace of mind.

Set A Standard For Yourself. Work according to a plan. Set a standard by which you will live. Do not have one which will prove a task to maintain, nor one which will not give you satisfaction as your present rolls into the past.

When evening comes and you can look back over a day which pleases you, it is quite certain—the standard you have decreed is a fitting one.

Live In Harmony. A prominent industrialist, when engaging an employee for an important position, will investigate the home-life as well as the ability and integrity of the applicant. He had found that employees with inharmony in the home were never as efficient as those who lived in an atmosphere of harmony.

As to peace of mind, it is easy to understand that there will be none in homes of bickering, nagging, and quarreling.

Making a success of your marriage is proving your leadership in directing one of the greatest institutions on the face of the earth.

Happiness in the home does not just happen. You have to plan for it. And the rewards are so compensating.

A man once told me that he is glad to leave home in the mornings and he dreads returning at night, due to marital inharmony. This man could not possibly have any peace of mind.

Another man told me he looked forward to returning to his home of love and harmony. You do not have to guess to know this one had peace of mind.

Finally, be conscious of your Peace of Mind. Cherish it to such an extent you will forever be grateful that you possess that which can easily be classed as the greatest blessing we can have in life.

Permit me to close this chapter with the thought so often expressed:

Happiness comes from giving happiness.

To those near and dear to you, help them to help themselves by teaching them the principles you have learned.

Summary

Everyone's ultimate objective is Peace of Mind. Without it, nothing else matters. You may have great riches and yet be miserable without Peace of Mind.

You have gained much from this book, I am sure. Probably, many times, as you would finish a chapter, you would say to yourself: "This chapter is worth far more than the cost of the book."

Now, here is what you can do to add still more value to your book. Read it all over again. You will not only read the lines—but with what you have already learned, you will read much between the lines. In other words, you'll be adding your own thinking to that of mine, making this work far more comprehensive.

I hope you have gained as much pleasure in reading "Add Years to Your Life, Life to Your Years" as I have had in preparing it for you.

And, may your added years be joyous years.

Knowledge Is of No Value Unless You Make Use of It

It is urged that you do not read this section until after you have read—and reread—the entire book.

Throughout this entire book, you have been given rules to follow, and you have been urged to follow them. Have you acted upon my advice? If you are an average individual, then the odds are against you.

A survey made some years ago indicated that only 25%—one out of four people—acted upon suggestions of a self-improvement nature.

Most people, when reading anything of this kind, will end by either saying to themselves: "Well that sounded good," or "I knew that all the time." But, no further thought is given to the material, nor any effort expended in putting the rules and formulas to work.

Sometimes, if a piece of work sounds good to us, we will think of Tom, Dick or Harry, who should have read it. But seldom do we look within to see if we, ourselves, might not be benefited.

Should you fall within the 75% category of those who gain but little from inspirational writings, do not feel unhappy about it. There is a basic reason why so few people are helped, one for which you might not even be responsible.

I am quite selfish, I guess. I so thoroughly enjoyed the countless hundreds of flattering letters I received from readers of my book: I CAN, I will not be happy unless the same thing happens with this book. I want you, and every other reader, to get so much from this book you will be unable to appraise in terms of dollars and cents its value to you.

To assure myself that this book will function for all readers as intended, this appendage has been added.

A Negative Mind Is the Destructive Factor

You were told that 75% of all people fail to gain materially from self-help instruction. Now I'll give you a figure more appalling: 95% of the population leans toward the negative side. Not all of these people are wholly negative; some of them are slightly so, on up to the unfortunate individual who is almost entirely negative in his thinking.

Practically all failure is due to negative thinking. A negative mind is responsible for most illness. Gloom and unhappiness are escorted into consciousness by a negative mind.

Do you understand how a negative mind functions?

It is subtle, very subtle. Without advance warning, the negative mind (and I am referring to the subconscious mind, because all conscious thinking is colored by the pattern established in the subconscious mind) will lead one toward negative conclusions. If you contemplate changing your job; a negative mind will warn you not to do so because you might not make good. If you yearn for a business of your own, you are steered from such a course by a negative subconscious mind which projects into consciousness the impression that you will surely fail.

If your mind is negatively controlled, the chances are that as you read this book, you wished you could add years to your life and life to your years, but your negative consciousness made you feel such blessings could not happen to you. Perhaps this does not apply to you. It this is true, wonderful! But, if you are guided by a negative mind, this last section of your book—if you will take it seriously—will change the picture for you. Then, after completing these final pages you will be asked to lay your book aside for two weeks, then read it again, and this time it will be with so much enthusiasm you'll have difficulty in holding yourself in check. You'll know you will add years to your life and life to your years.

Are You Naturally Negative?

We have heard that many people have halitosis without knowing it. This is true regarding a negative mind. It is amazing how many negative people we will encounter who declare, with definiteness, that they are not negative. They feel that the negative attitude is prompted by good judgment rather than through a reluctance engendered by an ingrained tendency to look on the negative side of everything.

To enable you to tell to what an extent you are negative, I am going to give you a test. It is a simple test, yet quite accurate. But, in order to reach a correct conclusion, you must adhere to the instructions right to the letter.

Here Is the Test!

First get a sheet of paper and a pen or pencil. Draw a line down the center of the page, then draw another line down the center of the right-hand half of the page. This will give you one wide column and two small ones. Over the top of one narrow column write the word "negative," and atop the other narrow column, the word "positive." I will give you several words. Take a word, and write it in the wide column. While writing it, note your reaction to it. I mean by this: The first impression to enter your mind before you have had a chance to think about it. If you first think about the word, you will create an impression based upon desire instead of fact.

As a simple illustration; suppose I should give you the word "Crag," what would come to your mind? What is the immediate impression you receive? A negative mind might conjure mental pictures of dangerous, precipitous heights; and might even imagine himself falling from a high place and being injured through contact with crags.

The positive mind would see beauty in the crags which added to the scenic value of mountains.

So, to properly take this test, do the following:

Write down the word in the wide column.

Think about it while writing it.

If you instinctively dislike the word, write "no" in the negative column. If you instinctively like the word, write "yes" in the positive column.

Now then, do you understand clearly how to make this test? All right, here are the words:

Clock
Money
Friend
Harmony
Guilt
Recreation
Mailman
Rain
Coffee
Love
Peace

Book
Happiness
Personality
Omen
Home
Grass
Police
Intelligence

If you have an even number of yes and no, you are in balance so far as your negative and positive tendencies are concerned. With such a mind you are not apt to accomplish anything outstanding in life due to your negative tendencies, yet you will not be a definite failure because of the positive characteristics you do possess.

If you have a big majority of "yes" notations, you can stop reading right now, because your future will be quite secure, and, so far as this book is concerned, already you have proved to yourself—conclusively—that you can add years to your life, and life to your years. In fact, by this time you have evidence that this is true.

If you have noted "no" to a majority of the words, well, you keep on reading.

To help you to better evaluate your spontaneous impressions, let us take each word individually for a brief analysis as to its negative and positive aspects.

Clock. Negatively; it could mean the passing of time, so far as death is concerned. Positively; it can remind us of pleasant things; important engagements, meal time, time for recreation, etc.

Money. Negatively; it could remind one of debts, lack, and responsibility. Positively; pleasure of making it, ability to give happiness to others.

Friend. Negatively; lack of friends, loneliness. Positively; companionship, someone who understands.

Harmony. Negatively; lack of it—inharmony, discord, quarreling. Positively; good music, pleasure, peace, enjoyment.

Right. Negatively; it might emphasize a feeling of inadequacy, making one feel he does nothing right. Positively; happiness in the thought that you do right toward your fellow man.

Guilt. Negatively; one's conscience reminds him of his mistakes and indiscretions. Positively; one gains a sense of peace that his mistakes have been forgiven.

Recreation. Negatively; one feels he has not done enough to have earned recreation. Positively; one feels how wonderful it is to have periods for recreation so that he can restore lost energy, making him more fit for his work.

Mailman. Negatively; one thinks of the bad news, bills, etc., brought by the mailman. Positively; one sees the mailman as a harbinger of glad tidings.

Rain. Negatively; wet and wrinkled clothing, catching colds, spoiled outings. Positively; purified atmosphere, grateful trees, shrubs, gardens.

Coffee. Negatively; sleeplessness, indigestion, heart effects. Positively; sociability, rest periods, pleasant beverage.

Love. Negatively; one senses a lack of love, either being received or given. Positively; a warm glow comes to the heart in memory of your love for others, and their love for you.

Peace. Negatively; strangely enough, one thinks of noise, confusion, disturbances of all kinds. Positively; one realizes how he is blessed with harmony and peace of mind.

Book. Negatively; many things come to mind, the book you borrowed and did not return, your bank book with nothing in it, the book or books, you owe for. Positively; you might see yourself cuddled up by a warm fire with a good book.

Happiness. Negatively; one pities himself for his lack of happiness. Positively; a warm glow encircles the heart in appreciation for the happiness which has come, and is coming, into his life.

Personality. Negatively; one views himself as being devoid of personality. Positively; one sees himself as being in intimate contact with those who possess a magnetic personality.

Omen. It is quite evident as to the type of mental pictures this word brings into mind. Negatively; a sign of bad luck. Positively; good luck.

Home. Unfortunately, to many, this word brings pictures of in-harmony, nagging, quarreling. To the positive minded, it portrays a haven of rest and harmony.

Grass. Negatively; the word, to many, means labor. Positively; life, beauty, recreation.

Police. Did the word bring a chill to your spine? It so, check the negative column. If you are positive, the word means law and order, protection, etc.

Intelligence. Negatively; this word points an accusing finger at an individual, intimating he lacks intelligence. Positively; one feels gratified that he can be classed as one of intelligence, and uses his reasoning faculties in proving it.

*   *   *

This test has been illuminating, I am sure. It may have been a surprise to many readers, who now realize they do lean toward the negative side.

But, even if you do find this to be true, do not worry about it. Negative minds can be changed to positive. Ten simple steps will now be given you which will lift you from the negative side to the positive, and in a comparatively short time.

1. Through reason, realize that the main difference between the one who succeeds and the one who fails is a matter of awareness. Think of those who are successful and in better than average good health, and you will recall to mind people who live on the positive side of life; men and women who eliminate the "t" from can't and make it "can!"

2. Life is a succession of habits. Nearly everything we do; every thought we think; are all reflecting habit patterns. A negative mind did not just happen. It is the result of continual negative thinking, much of which dates back to childhood. Begin changing your mental habit pattern by thinking in terms of: "I am positive in my thinking."

3. Think of that being of yours as being a separate entity from your mind. Consider yourself as mentor and that it is your duty to teach yourself positive thinking. If this were a fact instead of a fantasy, you would guard every thought which entered the mind. If a thought of illness, age, unhappiness, failure should seek entrance, you would at once eliminate it. So, guard your thoughts.

4. Watch your conversation. Put yourself on a routine of positive conversing. If others bring up negative subjects for conversation, offset them with a positive thought.

There are so many good things to talk about, it is unnecessary to be negative.

5. In writing letters, guard every word you use. Write positive letters. Say the things which will give happiness to the one reading your letter. This helps to give you a positive mind by training you to search for positive, helpful thoughts.

6. Start a positive thought file. Obtain a small filing box, something like a loose-leaf recipe file. Get a quantity of 3 x 5-inch filing cards. With an alphabetical index you are ready to begin "accentuating the positive." Take the letter "A" and think of every positive word which starts with that letter, such as active, alert, ambitious, amiable, etc. With the "B's" you will think of many words such as beauty, benevolent, brilliant, bountiful, etc. Take a card for each word and file it alphabetically. Every time you find an inspirational thought regarding any of your positive words, write it on the card. You might never refer to your file, but the act of compiling it has a tendency to fix the positive words in your mind.

7. Develop a tremendous enthusiasm for your developing positive mind. Be enthusiastic because already it is beginning to change your life for the better. Be so excited over the wonderful things which are coming into your life, you will never again allow yourself to dwell, even momentarily, on the negative side.

8. Teach others how to gain a positive mind. This is not suggested merely to make you generous. There is a definitely selfish reason why you should do this. One cannot successfully teach others to be

positive unless he, himself, has a positive mind. So, you will find yourself practicing what you preach. Students have frequently told me that this one suggestion proved more potent than any other. You will, too, the moment you put this step into action. When people begin commenting on how young you look (and they will as you follow the suggestions given in this book) you then have a golden opportunity to begin telling them how they, too, can add years to their lives and life to their years. This step is vitally important. Do not lose any time in taking advantage of what it can and will do for you.

9. Begin creating new habit patterns based upon these ten steps now. On the wall in my breakfast room, where I see it every morning as I start the new day, is a framed motto: "Every Day I'm On My Way!" This means that my path is ever onward and upward. I do not permit a day to pass without doing something of a constructive, or self-help nature. I do not wait until the end of the day to see if I did anything of a forward nature that day. No! While eating breakfast I decide on the positive things I will do that day. Then at night, as I prepare to retire, I can look back over a satisfactory day of accomplishment.

I am not implying that one should make a machine of himself and think of nothing except working at high speed and great efficiency at all times. One must have recreation, and the most worthwhile recreation is when it is planned. If we plan our days so that we can have time for enjoyable recreation, it will be enjoyed. If we work without a plan and wait to rest when we become tired, we will not benefit by the moments of leisure.

10. Be Happy. This sounds familiar to you because it is mentioned several times already in this book.

Happiness is positive, gloom, negative. Unless you can put yourself in a happy frame of mind, there is little chance of gaining from these or any other self-improvement principles.

A business executive once told me that each day before going to his office he takes steps to get himself in a happy frame of mind.

Problems of the day never disturb him because he knows he is master of them, instead of being mastered by them. His judgment is better, his decisions more correct when he has a happy mind. In other words, happiness pays off in a tangible way as well as making one merely feel good within.

Happiness particularly applies to age and a consciousness of age. When one approaches his mirror with an unhappy mind, his face looks older than when he does so with a glow of happiness. He leaves the mirror with the feeling that he is showing his age, and the more one dwells, mentally, on age, the more he accelerates the aging processes.

Finale!

Unless you were sincere in your desire to add years to your life, and life to your years, you would not be reading this book this far. But remember! Merely reading the book—no matter how interesting—is not enough. You must translate this knowledge into experience.

There are many books intended to teach you how to draw pictures. In fact, you could, in a single evening, learn how to draw, but you wouldn't become an artist until you made use of that knowledge.

Begin planning your future! Remember, you are going to live as though your life would go on forever. Lay out a series of objectives for yourself. Decide on what you want to happen for you this year. Consider the advancement you would like to make in the next five years, but go even further. What do you foresee for the distant future, say, twenty to twenty-five years?

As I told you in the beginning of this book, I have reached my 70th birthday. To many I might be thought of as an old man, but I so thoroughly live according to the principles I teach, I cannot see myself as anything but a young man. Physically I am better in every way than I was when 40, and I was considered a good physical specimen at that time.

The plans I have laid out for my future will take me well beyond the 100-year mark to accomplish.

"Kidding yourself," you might remark. All right, suppose that I am living a life of make-believe. Let me ask a question! If I live as if my life would go on forever, wouldn't I be happier than constantly dreading the passing of each day? Wouldn't my last years be happier than otherwise?

And, if I have a mind free from the fear of death, isn't it just sound reasoning to believe that I will live longer? Your good judgment must answer this in the affirmative.

Life has never been as exciting as it is now. Electronics are daily bringing new conveniences and enjoyment into the home. Modern air travel has reduced the transportation time between continents from weeks and days to mere hours. The use of atomic energy for industrial and home use, instead of for wholesale murder is rapidly becoming a fact. Travel to other planets is becoming a certainty of the foreseeable future.

With all that is happening and about to happen it would be easy to gain an age consciousness; feeling that we will not live long enough to see many of the great predictions come into reality.

But, if you live as though your life will go on forever, this will not happen to you. You will do as I have done. You will be at ease in the thought that you will be a part of the thrilling world of tomorrow.

Now, good reader, lay this book aside for two weeks. In the meantime think about it. Recall to mind everything you have read, or, at least as much of it as you can. See to it that you are practicing the principles you have remembered.

Then begin rereading the book from the very first page.

If you have profited by the ten steps given in this appendage, you will gain many times the good from this second reading as you did the first time.

Do not give your book away. Remember, you are changing habits formed throughout a lifetime. From time to time you will want to review many of the chapters contained in the book.

Now then, start adding years to your life and life to your years!

AFTERWORD

So what became of Ben Sweetland?

Dr. Sweetland wrote this book in 1958, the year he turned 70. One estimate put the life expectancy of American men born in 1888 who survived to age 5 at 62; so, at least statistically, he had already added years to his life. Dr. Sweetland died in 1963, one month before his 75th birthday. He didn't live forever (at least not in his physical body) but he surpassed the typical life expectancy of his time.

More important than the number of years in his life is the amount of life in his years. Dr. Sweetland followed his passions throughout his life. In the mid-1950's, he developed a sleep learning system that was widely adopted. According to his obituary, he continued traveling and speaking professionally in his later years and was working on a new book at the time of his death.

None of us know how many years we will have on this Earth. We can do what is in our power to make the best of our health, but there are no guarantees that we will live to an old age. The ideas shared by Dr. Sweetland may help you add years to your life. They will definitely add life to your years.

ABOUT SPECIAL INTERESTS PUBLISHING

Special Interests Publishing offers a variety of quality nonfiction titles. You can learn more about our books at our website, https://SIPub.com/.

We also publish a line of journals under our imprint, Journals to Write In. The journals come in a range of styles, including lined journals, bullet grid journals and specialty journals such as those for recipes, gratitude, goals and more. You can see all of our journals at our website, https://SIPub.com/journals and on Amazon.com at https://Amazon.com/author/journals.

Co-author Cathy Stucker is best known as The Idea Lady. She is an author, consultant and speaker who has helped thousands of people create the work and the life of their dreams. You can learn more about Cathy at https://IdeaLady.com/.

Do you have questions, comments or suggestions about any of our publications? Please feel free to contact the publisher directly at publisher@sipub.com.

Thank you for being one of our valued readers!

Made in United States
North Haven, CT
20 January 2023

31368768R00104